WAINWRIGHT

Self Expression and Conduct

The Humanities

RESEARCH, CURRICULUM, EVALUATION, AND WRITING

PAUL F. BRANDWEIN
Adjunct Professor, University of Pittsburgh
Member, The National Humanities Faculty

MARGARET COTTOM-WINSLOW
Research Associate
Center for the Study of Instruction
San Francisco, California

AGNES McCARTHY
Research Associate
Center for the Study of Instruction
San Francisco, California

RESEARCH AND DEVELOPMENT: SPECIAL MODES AND MATERIALS OF INSTRUCTION

RITA ABRAMS
Vocal and Choral Music
Mill Valley, California

PHILLIP DIZICK
Artist and Teacher
Mill Valley, California

LYN ELDER
Instrumental Music
San Francisco, California

MARGUERITE RENNA
Music Specialist, San Rafael City Schools
San Rafael, California

VIRGINIA TANNER
Director, Creative Dance
Division of Continuing Education
University of Utah

ALEX H. URBAN
Resource Specialist
Creative Dramatics and Dance
Vallejo, California

CORINNE WATSON
Reading Consultant
Center for the Study of Instruction
San Francisco, California

CONSULTING SCHOLARS IN THE HUMANITIES

ARTHUR D. AMIOTTE
Lakota Cultural Art Educator
Bureau of Indian Affairs
Manderson, South Dakota

CSI CENTER FOR THE STUDY OF INSTRUCTION
SAN FRANCISCO, CALIFORNIA

Self Expression and Conduct

The Humanities

RUDOLF ARNHEIM
Professor of the Psychology of Art
Harvard University

SAMUEL ELKIND
Professor of Theater Arts
California State University at San Francisco

BEN HAZARD
Curator of Special Exhibits and Education
The Oakland Museum
Oakland, California

JAMES JARRETT
Professor, School of Education
University of California at Berkeley

WILLIAM JOVANOVICH
Literature and Criticism

RICHARD McLANATHAN
Consultant in Art, National Gallery
Washington, D.C.

AMÉRICO PAREDES
Professor of English and Anthropology
University of Texas at Austin

JAMES BENNETT PRITCHARD
Associate Director, University Museum
University of Pennsylvania

MARTHA MAYBURY WAMPLER
Consultant and Teacher
Orff-Schulwerk Institute

RICHARD YEE
Associate Professor of Philosophy
Holy Names College
Oakland, California

SPECIAL DESIGN FOR INSTRUCTION:
CENTER FOR THE STUDY OF INSTRUCTION

ERIK ARNESEN
Photography

YIM GETMAN
Design

MADELINE TRAVERS HOVLAND
Research and Writing

ANN POTTER
Research and Art

NAHUM ZILBERBERG
Consultant

HARCOURT BRACE JOVANOVICH
NEW YORK CHICAGO SAN FRANCISCO ATLANTA DALLAS and LONDON

SPECIALISTS IN EDUCATION / CONSULTING TEACHERS / FIELD TESTING

MARGARET COMPTON
Cranford Public Schools
Cranford, New Jersey

JUANITA ELROD
R. A. Mitchell Elementary School
Gadsden, Alabama

NOREEN FORADORI
United Independent Schools
East Cleveland, Ohio

JANE LINDAMOOD
Charleston School
Lorain, Ohio

POLLY LONG
Aberdeen Elementary School
Aberdeen, North Carolina

DOROTHY MICHELSON
Illinois Park School
Elgin, Illinois

PATRICIA MURPHY
Oak Grove Elementary School
Bloomington, Minnesota

ALBERT A. RENNA
Director of Music
San Francisco Unified School District

NANCY T. SCOTT
Spartanburg City Schools
Spartanburg, South Carolina

THOMASSINE SELLERS
California State University
at San Francisco

ELISE SINGLETON
Leewood Elementary School
Miami, Florida

BETTY BOBB STRAUSS
Frostwood Elementary School
Houston, Texas

FAYE G. WALDRON
Music Specialist,
Lake Elementary School
Vermilion, Ohio

GEORGE L. WHITE
Consultant in Education
San Francisco, California

ISBN 0-15-373302-0

PRINTED IN THE UNITED STATES OF AMERICA

ACKNOWLEDGMENTS: For permission to reprint copyrighted material, grateful acknowledgment is made to the following sources: *Doubleday & Company, Inc.:* From *Birds, Frogs, And Moonlight,* translated by Sylvia Cassedy and Kunihiro Suetake, copyright © 1967 by Doubleday & Company, Inc. *Dover Publications, Inc.:* Adaptation of "Wai-kun," fable sung and told by Chash-chunk-a (Wave, Peter Sampson) from *The Indians' Book* edited by Natalie Curtis, copyright © 1907, 1923, 1934, 1950 by Paul Burlin. *Harcourt Brace Jovanovich, Inc.* and *Curtis Brown, Ltd.:* "Waterfall, only" from *More Cricket Songs: Japanese Haiku* translated by Harry Behn, copyright © 1971 by Harry Behn. *Harper & Row, Publishers, Inc.:* "Keziah" from *Bronzeville Boys And Girls* by Gwendolyn Brooks, copyright © 1956 by Gwendolyn Brooks Blakely. *Instructor, The Instructor Publications, Inc.:* From "The Haiku of Jack Franklens Camp" by Marion Wallace from *Instructor,* copyright © January 1973, *Little, Brown and Co.* and *Curtis Brown, Ltd.:* From "Every Time I Climb A Tree" from *Every Time I Climb A Tree* by David McCord, copyright 1952 by David McCord. *McGraw-Hill Book Company:* From *Springs Of African Wisdom,* edited by Erwin J. Haeberle, copyright 1970 Leobuchhandlung. *William Morrow & Company, Inc.:* "Beauty" from *I Am A Pueblo Indian Girl* by E-Yeh-Shure', copyright © 1939 by William Morrow & Company, Inc.; renewed, 1967 by Louise Abeita Chiwiwi. *The University of Chicago Press:* Excerpt adapted from *Kumulipo, A Hawaiian Creation Chant,* translated and edited by Martha W. Beckwith, copyright © 1951 The University of Chicago Press.

© Hildegard Steinmetz: page 15; © 1971 Publishers Hall Syndicate TMR: page 34 left; © 1974 King Features Syndicate: page 35 top, page 35 bottom; From *The Grandes Heures of Jean Duke of Berry* by Marcel Thomas, reprinted with permission of publisher George Braziller, Inc. and the *Bibliotheque Nationale:* page 50 left; Grandma Moses (Anna May Robinson Moses), "The Schoolhouse." Painted in 1949. Copyright 1949 by Grandma Moses Properties, Inc., New York.

PHOTOGRAPH ACKNOWLEDGMENTS

KEY: T, top; B, bottom; L, left; C, center; R, right.

HARBRACE: 2T, 3, 4, 7, 10, 11T, 16, 17, 19, 20, 21L, 24TR, 24C, 24BL, 24BR, 26, 28–29, 31TL, 31TR, 32TR, 32BL, 40–41, 43TR, 48TR, 48BL, 48BR, 51C, 51BR, 55, 56B, 57B, 58, 62, 63, 70, 73, 74, 75, 76–77, 85TL, 85B, 86TL, 86TC, 86CR, 86B, 91B, 97, 98, 99R, 104TR, 104CL, 104BR, 109, 110, 111T, 115T, 115BL, 116, 117, 119, 121TL, 121C, 124–125, 127BR, 128TL, 128TR, 128BR, 130, 133L, 136–137, 139TR, 146TR, 146BL, 147T, 148–149, 151TL, 151B, 153, 154, 155TL, 156–157, 159R, 160, 161, 164, 165, 170, 171B, 172TL, 172BL, 173, 178–179, 181T, 181BL, 182–183, 186L, 189B, 190–191, 193, 196BL, 196BR, 201BL, 202–203, 205TL, 205TR, 206L, 206TR, 207, 214–215, 217, 218T, 219, 220, 223T, 223BR, 225TL, 225TR, 225BC, 225BR, 232–233, 235, 236, 237B, 238TL, 238TR, 247B, 248BC, 249C, 255, 256–257, 259TL, 260, 262TR, 262BL, 262BR, 263TR, 268–269, 271, 274, 275, 276.

HARBRACE by Eileen Christelow: 61BL, 61BR, 86TR, 121R, 151TR, 155TR, 155BL, 155BR, 159L, 171TL.

HARBRACE by Jacques Jangoux: 101–102, 239.

HARBRACE by Phiz Mezey: 48TL, 61T, 181BR, 201CL, 201BR, 238BL.

HARBRACE by J. Oliver Mitchell: 21R.

HARBRACE by Janet Mohr: 102TR.

HARBRACE by Loli Nakamoto: 211.

HARBRACE by Bob Powals: 80B, 80R, 86CL, 139TL, 139B, 169BR, 171TR, 172TR, 206B, 247TR, 259TR.

HARBRACE by David Powers: 43TL, 43B, 91T, 102BL, 103TR, 105CR, 105BL, 205B.

HARBRACE by Richard Reeves: 11B, 24TL, 31B, 32BR, 51TL, 51TR, 51BL, 99L, 104TL, 105TR, 105BR, 121BL, 146C, 147C, 171CR, 247TL, 248BL, 263B.

HARBRACE by William Rosenthal: courtesy of Judas Magnes Museum, 50R.

HARBRACE by Tom Tracy: 2B, 56T, 80T, 80C, 80BL, 82–83, 85TR, 112, 115BR, 133C, 163, 169T, 169BL, 172BR, 186R, 189T, 194–195, 224, 225BL, 237T, 238BR, 249B, 259B, 261, 262TL.

HARBRACE, courtesy of: Hoover Art Gallery, San Francisco, California. "Nob Hill and Treasure Island" by Dong Kingman: 67B; Bill Hyde: 127BL; Robert H. Lowie Museum, Berkeley, California: 13, 27B; Ringling Bros. and Barnum & Bailey Circus: 1, 57T, 111B, 166, 218B, 225TC, 272; San Francisco Art Institute: 223BL; San Francisco Police Department: 133R; San Francisco Police Department Athletic League: 32TR; the Toronto Dominion Bank, Toronto, Canada and The Fine Arts Museum of San Francisco, M.H. de Young Memorial Museum, "Small Man with Drum," Oknickitakah from the Canadian Arts Council, "Man with Drum," Tesenkit (?), "Archer," Isa Smiler, "Hunter with Bird Spear" artist unknown: 228.

RESEARCH CREDITS: Robert Graham: 12; the Robert H. Lowie Museum of Anthropology, Berkeley, California: 13TR, 13B; Museum of the American Indian, Heye Foundation, New York: 27TL, 27TR; Gene Harris, Meyers Photo-Art: 37; Jerry Freidland: 38, 39; Lisa Little, Museum of Primitive Art: 47; Yeshiva University Museum: 49TL; Harrison Forman: 49TC, 49BC; Paolo Koch, Rapho-Guillumette: 49TR, 49BL; Louis Goldman, Rapho-Guillumette: 49BR; Nelson Gallery, Atkins Museum, Kansas City, Missouri: 65; "The Fog Warning" by Winslow Homer, courtesy of the Museum of Fine Arts, Boston, Massachusetts: 67T; Ballet Folklorico of Mexico, courtesy of Hurok Concerts, Inc.: 78; Harrison Forman: 79TL, 79BR; Fred Lyon, Rapho-Guillumette: 79TR; Sabine Weiss, Rapho-Guillumette: 79BL; Arthur Amiotte: 81; Owen Franken, Stock, Boston: 89TL, 89BL, Jacques Jangoux: 89TC; Elliot Erwitt, Magnum: 89TR; William Carter: 89BC; Rene Burri, Magnum: 89BR; Historical Pictures Service: 90C; Marilyn Silverstone, Magnum: 102TL; Owen Franken, Stock, Boston: 102BR; Hedrich-Blessing: 103TL; Harrison Forman: 103BL; BBM Associates: 103BR; Stock, Boston: 104 CR; United States Department of the Interior, National Park Service, Cape Cod National Seashore: 104BL; United States Department of the Interior, National Park Service, Saguaro National Monument: 105TR; United States Department of the Interior, National Park Service, Cape Cod National Seashore: 105CL; Collection of the Whitney Museum of American Art. Gift of Howard and Jean Lipman Foundation, Inc.: 118; Bancroft Library, Berkeley, California: 122, 123L; Kodansha, Ltd. and the National Institute of Anthropology and History, Mexico City: 123R; NASA: 127T; Alec Duncan: 128BL; Culver Pictures, Inc.: 131; Marvin Silverman: 135; The Viking Museum: 142; The Metropolitan Museum of Art, Anonymous and Gift, 1944: 143; NASA: 146TL; Ron and Joyce Church: 146–147B; Terry Eiler: 176; Supp Seitz, Magnum: 196TL; Russell Abraham: 196TR; The California Milk Advisory Board: 201T; Adler Planetarium: 208–209; United States Department of the Interior, National Park Service: 210TL; Mr. and Mrs. Hiram L. Parent: 201BL; John Hovland: 210R; Hi Enterprises: 213; Terry Eiler: 226T; Gene Harris, Meyers Photo-Art: 226B; Jacques Jangoux: 227TL, 227BL; Don Kline: 227TR; William Apton: 227BR; D. Wilkinson, Information Canada Photothêque: 228L; "Winter River Landscape," the Asian Art Museum of San Francisco, the Avery Brundage Collection: 243; Jon Lewis: 248 Row 1L; Owen Franken, Stock, Boston: 248 Row 1C; UPI: 248 Row 1R; UPI: 248, Row 2L; Marilyn Silverstone, Magnum: 248 Row 2C; UPI: 248 Row 2R; UPI: 249T; Kanoke, Orion/BBM Associates: 250; "Battle between Genji and Heike," the Asian Art Museum of San Francisco, the Avery Brundage Collection: 251T; Orion/BBM Associates: 251BL, 251BR; Culver Pictures, Inc.: 254; Owen Franken, Stock, Boston: 263TL; Pictorial Parade: 267T; Morath, Magnum: 267B.

COVER CREDITS: Front, clockwise from TC, Harbrace; Harbrace by Eileen Christelow; Harbrace; Harbrace; Harbrace by Richard Reeves. Back, clockwise from TC, Nancy Freeman (detail); Liisa Rahkonen (detail); Bob Tamura (detail); Rosemary Deasy (detail); Bonnie Brown (detail).

ART ACKNOWLEDGMENTS

Jean Backer: 240; Bonnie Brown: ixT, 167, 168; Art Cummings: 132; Rosemary Deasy: ixB, 221, 222; Tom Durfee: 8–9 Row 1; Nancy Freeman: vii, 5, 6; David Grove: 158; Keith Halonen: 144, 145, 184, 188: used by permission of Regina Kane: 229; John Kuzich: 18, 30, 42, 54, 72, 84, 96, 108, 126, 138, 150, 162, 180, 192, 204, 216, 234, 246, 258, 270; Bill Morrison: 252, 253, 264; Liisa Rahkonen: viiiB, 8–9 Row 3, 113, 114, 197; Frank Remciewicz: 8–9 Row 2, 25, 35L, 174–175; Gretchen Schields: 45; Robert Tamura; viiiT, 59, 60, 92, 140–141, 241; Jack Tom: 198, 199.

Grateful acknowledgment is made to the following schools for their help in obtaining photographs and children's artwork: Nannie Smith Berry Elementary School, City of Hendersonville, Tennessee; Cathedral Grammar School, Boston, Massachusetts; Discovery Center, San Francisco, California; Holden Art Center, Charlottesville, Virginia; Jackson-Via Elementary School, City of Charlottesville, Virginia; Le Conte School, Berkeley, California; McCleary Elementary School, McCleary, Washington; Marin Terrace Elementary School, Mill Valley, California; Oakland Unified School District, Lincoln School, Oakland, California; George Peabody School, San Francisco, California; Redwood Heights School, Oakland, California; St. Patrick's Elementary School, York, Pennsylvania; San Antonio Independent School District, David Barkley Elementary School; Santa Clara Day School, Santa Clara Pueblo, New Mexico; Wilson School, Wilson, Wyoming.

CONTENTS

Do you know someone who is a good dancer? Do you know someone who makes beautiful things? Do you know someone who has a way with animals? What do *you* do best?

How good it feels to do something well! This book will tell you about many things you can make and do. Perhaps you will find something that you will begin to do well.

First, meet some boys and girls your age. They found something that they like to do. They will tell you how they began. Are you ready to begin?

WE BEGIN

My name is Sascha Cort. Sascha is short for Alexander. My family is with the Ringling Brothers and Barnum and Bailey circus. My father and grandfather are both clowns. Can you guess what I want to be some day?

I'm Denise Kill. I have two horses. I take care of them by myself. My big sister helps me sometimes. She told me about 4-H. I am joining 4-H this year. I want to show a horse at the County Fair. There will be prizes for the best animals.

Everyone calls me Lupe. My real name is Guadalupe Guerrero. My father plays the accordion. He has his own band. He is saying he will teach me to play the accordion, too!

I'm Bruce Wong, the boy at the left. I love to do folk dances. My teacher is showing us how to do part of a folk dance. Some day I'd like to be a really good dancer.

Eileen Naranjo is my name.
Taking pictures is my game.
I like to write poems too.
I write and draw about
what people do.

This is my teacher. She knows so much about taking pictures. I'm going to learn a lot this year.

My name is Benita Terrell. I live in Virginia. My mom and I like to go shopping. One day I saw this art store. Beautiful bowls made of clay were for sale. I'd love to learn how to make things from clay.

WAYS OF CARING

These are all ways of caring. People show that they care in many different ways.

Caring can be a warm, beautiful feeling. What do you care about?

How Do You Feel?

You land on the moon. You are all alone. What's that shadow moving toward you?

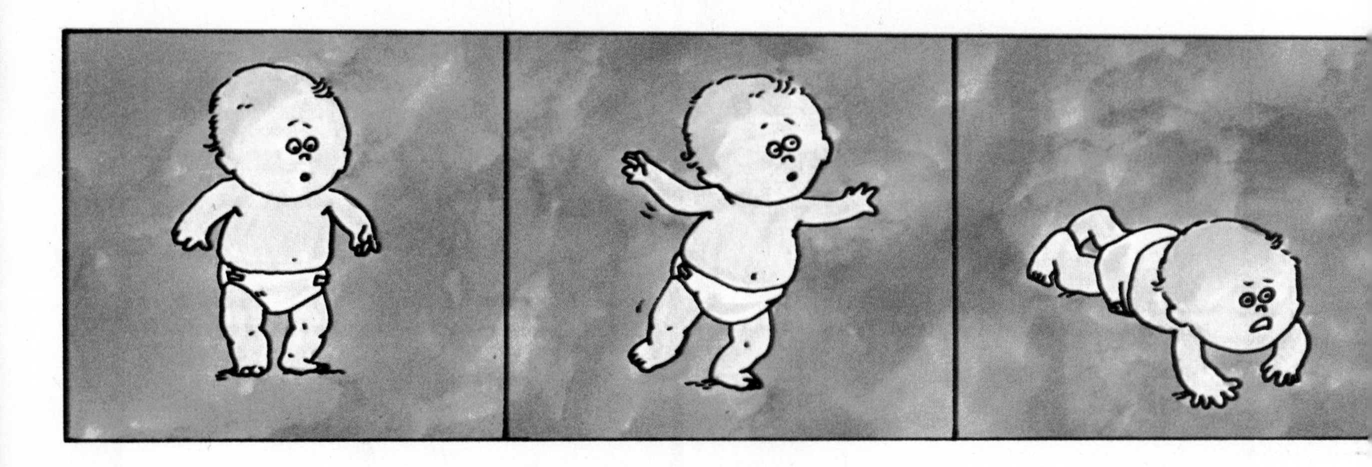

You are just learning to walk. How does it feel to stand by yourself? Oh, no! Down again! Then your brother helps.

You are lost and cold. Then you hear your father calling. At last you are safe at home.

Make believe you are in each row of pictures. How do you feel in the first picture? How do you feel in the last picture? Show how your feelings change.

Perhaps you will make up a *pantomime* (PAN·tuh·miym) to show feelings. In a pantomime you act out a story. You use your whole body. You don't use words.

Get together with some other children. First, decide what feelings you want to show. Then decide what would make your feelings change.

Act out what happens. Use your whole body. Be sure to show where you are. Are you on a bus? Are you under water?

Can the class guess what is happening? Ask the class to guess the feelings you are *pantomiming*.

You can show feelings with your body. Faces show feelings too.

Make a Face

Try making faces at home. Look in a mirror. Make the angriest face you can. Make a funny face. Make a happy face. Make a sad face. What other faces will you make?

Do some parts of your face show feelings better than other parts? Try showing each feeling with your eyes only. Then try showing each feeling with your mouth only.

Now, in school, take turns making faces. Make a face. Ask a friend to answer with a different face. Then show how your friend's face makes you feel. How many faces can the two of you make in a row without laughing?

Your face and your body show how you feel. Sometimes you can hide your true feelings. Have you ever done that? How does hiding feelings make you feel?

When you wear a mask, you hide your true feelings. A mask can show a different feeling than you have. Behind a mask of a sad face, you can be laughing.

Do you want to find out more about masks? Just turn the page!

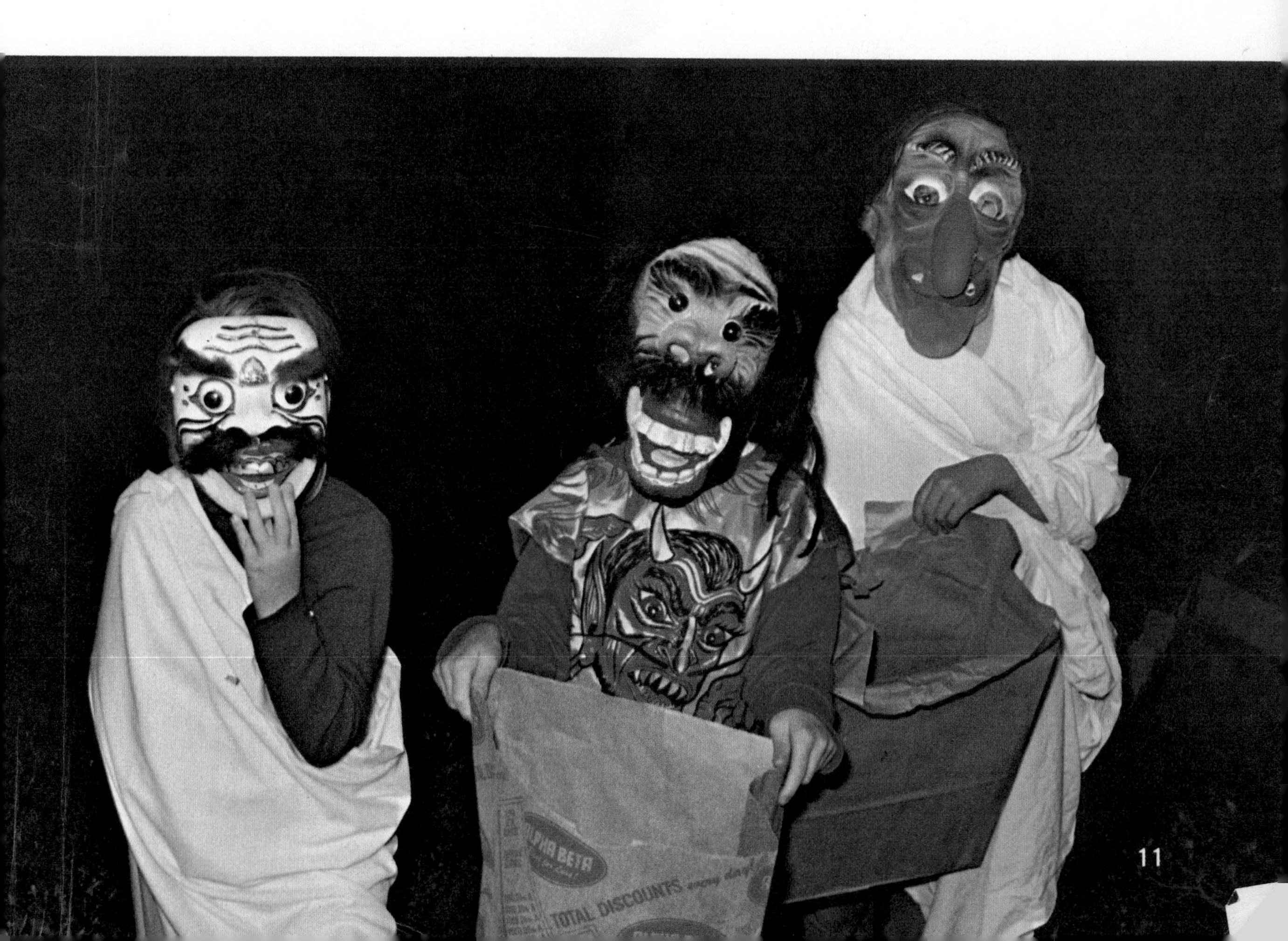

Sometimes masks look almost like real faces. Sometimes parts of the mask-face are *exaggerated* (ig·ZAJ·uh·rayt·ed) in some way. The eyes might look different from real eyes. The mouth or nose might be in a different place. Why do you think the mask-maker does that?

Exaggerated means bigger than in real life.

The masks on this page are from *Japan*. They are used in plays. How are these masks different from real faces? What feeling does each mask show? How are the feelings exaggerated?

Do you know where *Japan* is? Please find it on a map.

People all over the world make masks. These are Eskimo finger masks and face masks. Which are finger masks? How can you tell?

Shamans (SHAH·muhns) and their helpers used to make face masks. The Eskimos believed that a shaman could heal sick people. They thought he or she could see spirits in dreams.

The shamans made masks that looked like the spirits they saw. They put on a mask when they healed people. They put on a mask when they asked the spirits for help.

Eskimos use masks to tell stories too. Some Eskimos use finger masks when they dance.

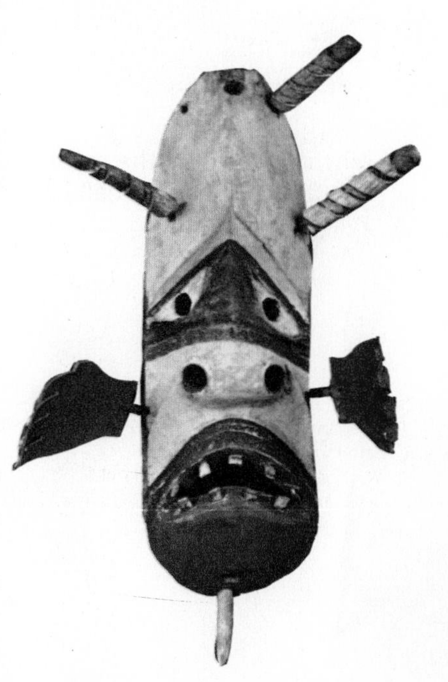

Masks and Make-Believe

Some people use masks to help them make believe. Sometimes they use masks in plays. When you act in a play, you make believe. You make believe you are angry. You make believe you are sad. Some feelings are easier to make believe than others. What feelings are easy for you to make believe?

All over the world people act in plays. Even more people watch plays. Why do you think so many people like to make believe?

Do you know where *Europe* is? Please find it on a map.

In *Europe* (U·ruhp), about five hundred years ago, many plays taught about good and evil. The main *character* (KAR·ik·tur) in one play was called *Everyman*.

A *character* is a person in a play or a story.

The other characters stood for things that were important to Everyman. On the next page, you can see what the characters stood for. Which person is wearing a mask?

Why do you think the main character was called *Everyman*?

The people were scared when Death tried to drag Everyman away. They were delighted when the play ended happily. They knew that the play was make-believe. Yet it seemed to tell about their real lives too.

Have you seen plays that seemed to tell about your life? What kind of television play do you like best? Have you ever liked a play that scared you?

Friendship
Family
Money
Devil
Death

SELF EXPRESSION

IN THE NORTHEAST

In Boston, Massachusetts, a class made up a play about Everyman. They wrote about the kind of person Everyman was. Then they made up other characters.

One character stood for Litter. He is wearing a litter mask. The sheet at the bottom shows litter, too. In the play, litter kills flowers. What do you think Everyman did then?

Perhaps your class will make up a play. Will you teach about good and evil in your play?

You might have each character stand for a feeling. Think about feelings you like. Think about feelings you don't like. How will each character look and act?

Do you have music *instruments* in your classroom? You might have each character choose a different instrument. Then the characters could "speak" in music instead of words.

You might want to invite people to see your play. How will you invite them?

Jj Kk Ll
scared

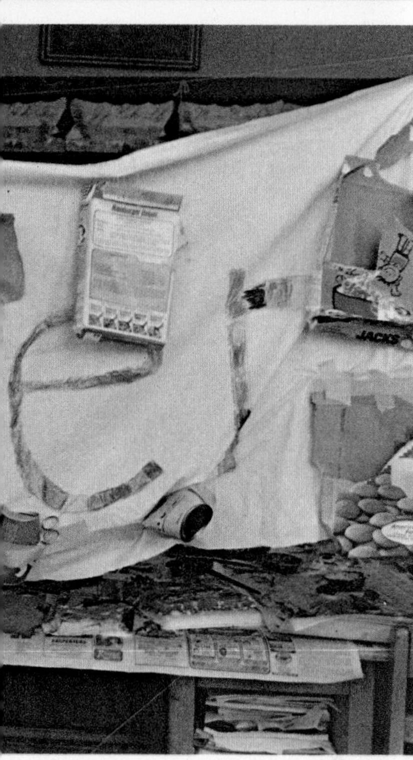
JACKS

Other Things to Try

You might want to tell a story about caring. Who will be in your story? What will they care about? Maybe the people will have more than one kind of feeling. What will they say? What will they do? You may tell your story in pictures or in words.

Here is the way a dance story might begin. Long ago, there was a king called *Ing*. The people in his land had names like *Running, Jumping,* and *Swinging*. One day some visitors came from the land of *Ly*. *Angrily, Sadly,* and *Lonely* made fun of the happy *Ing* people. What do you think happened? Will you make up a dance to tell about it?

Self Study

1 Do you think babies have the same feelings you have? Do old people have the same feelings you have? How can you show love for a baby? How can you show love for a grandmother?

2 How many different feelings do you have in one day? See if you can count them. Suppose people's feelings never changed. What would the world be like then?

People who really know you love you.
Who knows you best?

About Families

Why does the girl in this poem want to be alone?

KEZIAH

I have a secret place to go,
Not anyone may know.
And sometimes when the wind is rough
I cannot get there fast enough.
And sometimes when my mother
Is scolding my big brother,
My secret place, it seems to me,
Is quite the only place to be.

—Gwendolyn Brooks

Your face and body tell how you feel. Sometimes people write poems to tell how they feel. Sometimes they paint. How do *you* like to share feelings?

It often feels good to share feelings. In the poem, Keziah wants to be alone. When do you like to be alone? When do you like to be with others?

Suppose you had a secret place. What would it be like? Perhaps you will paint a picture of a secret place.

If you want to, you may share your picture. Do you want to keep your secret place a real secret? Then you'd better not share it.

With whom do you share secrets? How do you decide whom to trust?

Families and Feelings

Do you think you might ever want to live all alone? What might be some good things about living alone? What might be some things you would not like about living alone?

Most people live with other people. All over the world people live in families. There are many different kinds of families.

You may live with both parents. You may have brothers and sisters. Perhaps you live with just one person.

The people that you live with can make you angry sometimes. They can make you very happy sometimes. That's because you care about them. You care about how they feel. They care about you, too.

How many of your *relatives* have you met? Relatives are people who belong to your family. How many relatives do you know about? Perhaps you will draw a chart of your family. First, list the people with whom you live. Then write down the names of other relatives.

Ruth, Charlene, and Frank did the charts on this page. How will you do your chart? Perhaps you will show how each person in your family is *related* to you.

Do some of the people in your family live in other places? Perhaps you will write where they live, too.

People in a family may use words to tell how they feel. Sometimes they don't use words. Look at these pictures. How can you tell what the people feel?

What does a smile say? What does a tear say? What does a frown say?

Suppose you are feeling sad. Then someone you love smiles at you. How does that make you feel?

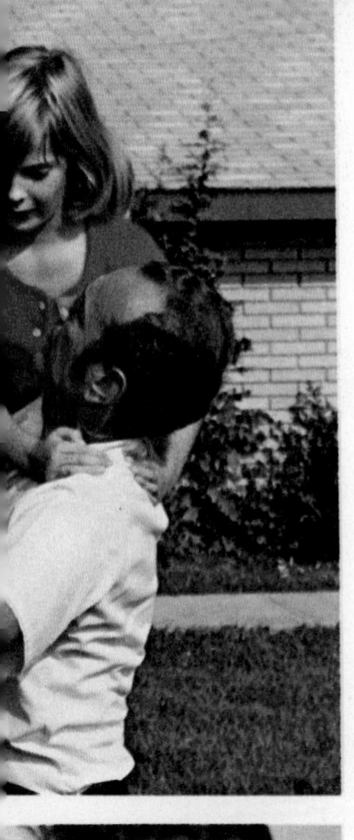

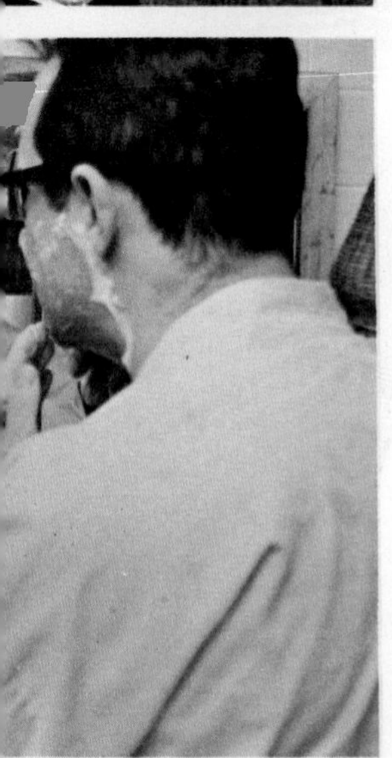

You might act out how people change one another's feelings. Choose a girl to be the mother. Choose a boy to be the father. Let other people play children's parts. The group should decide how old each child is. Give names to everyone, too.

Decide together what the family will be doing. What time of day will it be? Decide how you want the mother and father to feel. Here are some ideas.

happy

busy

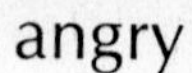

angry

hungry

Suppose that the children want to change their parents' feelings. What might they do to make their parents feel worse? What might they do to make them feel better?

History on Poles

Funny, sad, and exciting things happen to any family. Every family has a history. The history is made up of what has happened to the people in the family. It is also about what happened to the *ancestors* (AN·ses·turs) of the family. You might have the names of some ancestors on your chart.

Some Indians in North America used totem (TOH·tuhm) poles to tell about their families.

Your *ancestors* are your parents' parents. They are all of *their* parents, too.

The poles were made of wood. Every line carved into the pole had a meaning. The colors and lines told the family's history.

This pole was carved by Kwakiutl (kwah·kee·OO·tl) Indians. The Kwakiutls live in southwestern Canada.

You can see that animals were very important to this family. Animals may have helped the family in some way.

Some American Indians believed that their first ancestors were animal spirits. All of the people who came from the bear spirit belonged to the bear *clan*. The bear clan believed that the bear spirit had given the clan special power. The bear spirit had also given the clan special work to do.

A *clan* is a large group of relatives.

Kwakiutl Indians carved these animals, too. How do you think they felt about animals? How do you feel about animals?

SELF EXPRESSION

If you like, you may make a totem pole. Wood is hard to carve. Instead, you might want to cover boxes and cans with papier-mâché (PAY·pur·muh·SHAY). Then you can paint on the papier-mâché.

Papier-mâché is made from paper and paste. Your teacher will tell you how to make it.

You might tell about true history on your pole. You might want to make up a family history.

Perhaps you will make believe that an animal spirit has given your family special power. Which animal will you choose?

You don't have to paint the whole animal on your pole. If you are making a bird, make just the wings or the eyes. On a totem pole, part of an animal often stands for the whole animal.

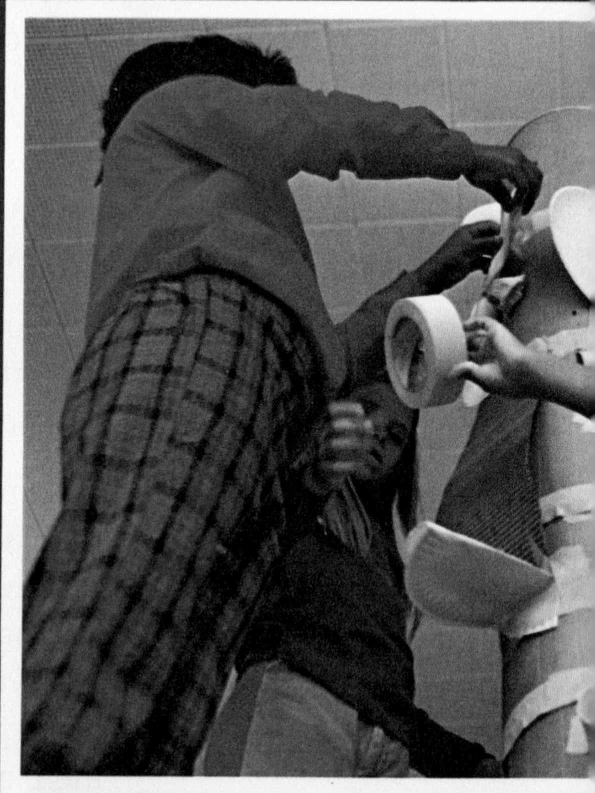

Other Things to Try

Perhaps you will write a *description* (di·SKRIP·shun) of your brother or sister. You don't have a brother or sister? Perhaps you will describe a brother or sister you would like to have.

A *description* is a picture in words. When you describe, you tell about something.

Are you working on an Everyman play? If so, you might want to have some people *mime* (MIYM) their parts. To see what that is like, try not using words for a while. Let your family know before you try it. How well do people at home understand your *miming*?

To *mime* means to act without words. *Mime* is short for *pantomime*.

Self Study

1. Suppose you were a parent. You want your child to grow up to be a fine, caring person. How would you bring up your child? What if your child cares about different things than you care about? What will you do or say?

2. When you are a grandparent, how do you think people will live? Will families be the same as they are today? How do you hope they will be?

How do friends help you become you?

Your Friends

Whom do you like to be with? Which person would you most like to be with at these times?

when you play outside
when you feel sick
when you learn about rocks
when you take your first plane ride

Did you think of the same person every time? Why do you like each of your friends?

You can find friends almost anywhere. Here are some places people find friends.

Goerge Peabody School,
Jan. 23, 1974

Dear Friend,

I have long black hair. I am brown. I have blue eyes and I am eight years old. I like to have pajama parties and I like to play kick ball. I have one sister and she is six. I like Christmas most of all, but I like to go camping and skating with my friends. I am in the third grade.

your friend,
Bonita.

Another way to make friends is by writing letters. Maybe you will write to someone in the United States. You might write to someone in a different country. Your teacher will tell you how to get a pen pal.

How will your pen pal be different from your other friends?

What kind of friend do you think would be best to have? Perhaps you will be that kind of friend to someone.

"AND THAT'S CALLED A *RAZZBERRY!*"

You will meet thousands of people during your life. Some of them will become your friends.

Do you think most people have the same friends all their lives? How do you make friends? How might you lose friends?

Sometimes people lose friends when they tease them. When do you like to be teased? When does it make you angry?

Sometimes people tease by giving their friends nicknames. Do you have a nickname? How do you like it? Some names can make people feel bad. Some names are fun to have.

Look at each picture. Which children feel hurt because of teasing? How can you tell? What do you do when you feel hurt?

Finding Out About Names

Names have always been very important to people. In some places, people keep their real names a secret. They think that if people know your name they have power over you.

How many names do you have? Some people have four or five names. Others have two names, a first name and a family name.

Some family names tell what job an *ancestor* had. Camilla Smith's ancestor made or fixed things. (Long ago a "smith" was a "maker.") Other names tell where an ancestor came from. Hovland is a Norwegian (nor WEE gen) name that means "land of Hov." What does a family name like Johnson tell?

Do you remember what an *ancestor* is? Please see page 26 if you don't.

Family names often come from a different language. They may be spelled differently today. That is why it is often difficult to tell what a family name means.

Most first names come from another language. Carmen comes from a Spanish word meaning "song." Alexander comes from Greek words meaning "helper of mankind." Mai Ling (MAY LEENG) is a Chinese name. It means "beautiful."

Do you know where *Norway*, *Spain*, *Greece*, and *China* are? Please find them on a map.

How did your family choose your name? Were you named for a relative? Does your name mean something?

Yoshiko (yo·SHEE·ko) is a Japanese name. At the right you can see it written in Japanese letters. This girl is writing her name with care and love. She writes her name over and over. She wants her name to look beautiful.

住子

Other children used letters that you use. They made their names look beautiful. You might try writing a name with care and love. Perhaps you will write the name of a friend.

Praise Names in Africa

Please find Nigeria on a map of the world.

Abionia (ah·BEE·oh·nah) means "born during a journey."

Ayoka (ah·yoh·KAH) means "one who causes joy all around."

Akin (a·KEEN) is a praise name that means "brave boy."

The Yoruba (YOH·roo·buh) people live in western *Nigeria* (niy·JIR·ee·uh) in Africa. Each Yoruba child has three names.

The first name tells about the child's birth. The second name has meaning mostly for the mother and father. The third name makes a wish for the child. This third name is the child's first praise name.

Praise names tell about the good things the Yoruba have done with their lives. Praise names may tell how a Yoruba looks. They may tell what he or she likes to do. By the time the Yoruba are old, they have many praise names.

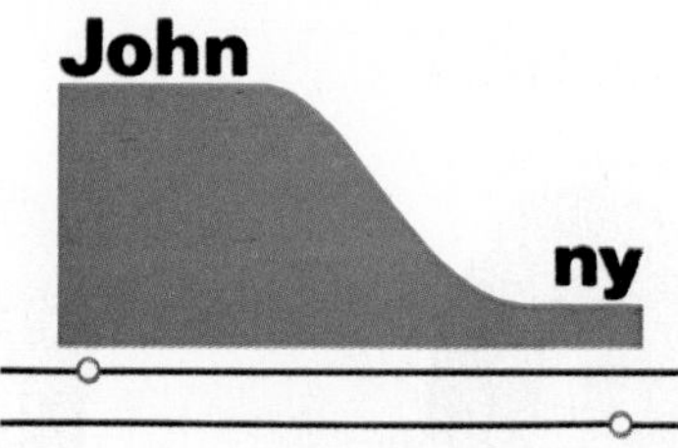

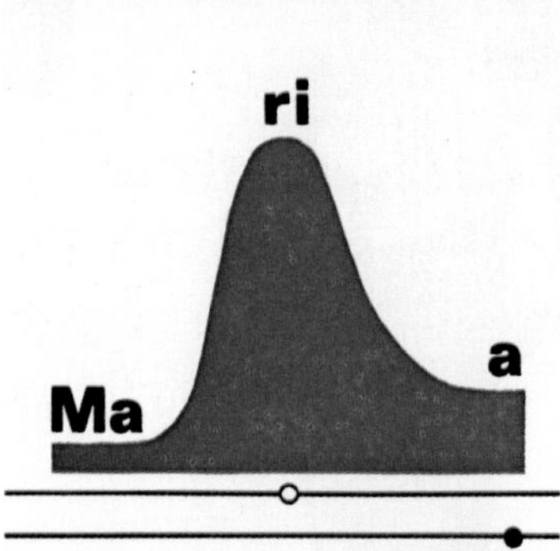

Chanting is singing a very simple tune. A chant may have just one or two pitches in it.

Drummers play and sing praise names at parties. They play the names on "talking drums." There are many kinds of talking drums. Talking drums sound like the Yoruba language.

The Yoruba language has three tones, or *pitches*. In Yoruba the same word might mean many different things. The meaning of a word depends on its pitch. Different pitches make the Yoruba language sound very much like singing.

Talking drums have many different pitches. How can that be? Can you make a drum that has two different pitches?

Sometimes your voice goes up and down in different pitches. Try *chanting* your name in two pitches. Can you do it in three pitches?

SELF EXPRESSION

Perhaps you will make up a dance about yourself and your friends. Kevin is showing how his name sounds. Sue is telling about her friend.

Think about what your name means. How will you show that in your dance?

Ask your friends to give you some praise names. Here are some ideas.

She can run very fast.

He likes to read.

Try saying each praise name in different ways. You can make your voice go up and down. You can stretch words. When you say those words, you can stretch with your whole self.

Think about ways to move that tell about your friends. Move in a way that tells how your friends make you feel. What will you choose to do?

VIN
BROWN
IS A
HELPING
FRIEND

Other Things to Try

Make a *montage* (mon·TAHZH) about friendship. You can cut parts of pictures from magazines. You can draw some pictures, too. Find or draw pictures that mean friendship to you. Arrange your pictures on paper. Then paste them down.

A *montage* is a picture made from pieces of pictures. The parts of the montage are pasted on a larger piece of paper.

Make believe you are a new girl or boy in school. Mime what happens when everyone is friendly to you. Now suppose that everyone is unfriendly. How will you show what happens?

You can dance part of your Everyman play. A dance might help to tell about friendship. What would that dance be like?

Self Study

1. Suppose you could choose anyone in the world to be your friend. Whom would you choose? Why would you choose him or her?

2. Suppose you have just met someone. You want that person to be your friend. What will you say? How will you act?

People you may not know care about you. How do these pictures show caring?

You and Everyone Else

Suppose you came to this town. You are on the crowded street in this picture. People and cars are all around you.

What kind of town have you reached? How can you tell if the people are kind to one another? What kind acts do you see?

Sounds show caring, too. What caring sounds do you hear in this town? What sounds do people make when they do *not* care?

Perhaps you will draw a picture to show a town you would like. You might also tape record sounds that tell about a town. If you tape sounds, perhaps you will have a radio show.

DR. DAY
MAIN ST.
MARKET
ICE CREAM
100
FLAVORS
MAIN
OAK
SCHIELDS.

Songs and Feelings

Suppose you heard singing in the streets of a town. Songs tell about all kinds of feelings. What songs do you like to hear?

Both "Kumbaya" (kum·buh·YAH) and "Hush, Little Baby" are *lullabies*. "Kumbaya" came from Africa a long time ago. "Hush, Little Baby" came from Europe.

Lullabies are songs sung to put a baby to sleep.

All over the world people sing lullabies to babies. Mothers and fathers want babies to feel safe. They want babies to feel they are loved.

Melodies are tunes.

Have you heard these *melodies* (MEL·uh·dees) before? Were the words the same? How were they different? Why do you think such old songs are still sung today?

Sing each lullaby. Clap where you see a different color in the words. Did you sing the songs fast or did you sing them slowly? Did you sing them loudly or softly?

Suppose you were singing the songs to a baby. How would you sing them? Softly clap the rhythm of the words as you sing. How would you dance to this music?

Can you make up new words with the same melodies? What will your words tell about? How will your songs make the baby feel?

KUM-BA YA YA
KUM-BA YA KUM-BA
YA YA KUM-BA YA
KUM-BA YA YA
KUM-BA YA AH AH
KUM-BA YA AH AH
KUM-BA YA

Signs of Caring

A song can show caring. A song can last for hundreds and hundreds of years.

You can see signs of caring all around you. Sometimes buildings show caring. How do parks and playgrounds show caring?

All of these buildings are very old. They have lasted for hundreds of years. What is the oldest building you have seen?

What did the people who built these buildings care about? How can you tell?

Lighting Up a Book

The pictures on these pages come from *illuminated* (i·LOO·muh·nay·ted) *manuscripts* (MAN·yuh·skripts). Illuminated manuscripts are books that were written by hand.

Illuminated means lit up. When you *illuminate* a room, you turn the light on.

Gold and silver paint were often used. The paint seemed to "light up" each page.

Books today are printed. Thousands of books are made at the same time. Long ago, artists lettered each book by hand. They painted pictures in the books. They decorated some letters with beautiful colors.

These manuscripts are hundreds of years old. How do they show love and caring?

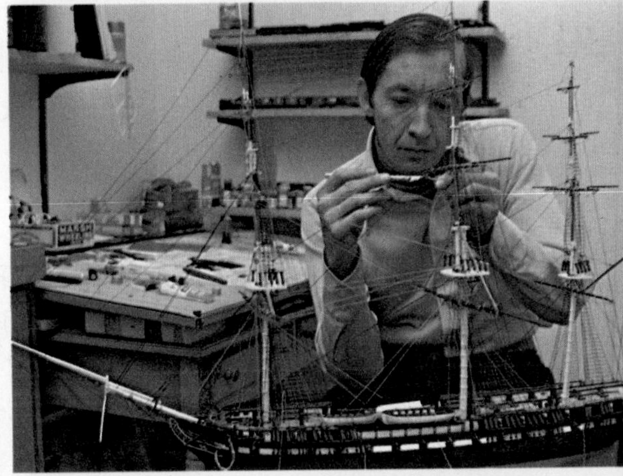

People in families hand down things, too. They make things with love and care. They want them to last for years and years.

If you have children, what beautiful things will you want to hand down?

SELF EXPRESSION

Perhaps you will make something that will last for a long time. Perhaps you will make a Caring Book. Will you do this alone or with others?

Look around your town. Find sights and sounds that show caring. Then decide how you will tell about them.

Perhaps you will draw pictures. Perhaps you will write about the things you see. You might want to try illuminating your writing with pictures and colors.

Some children in California made a Caring Book. Here are some pages from their book. When their book was finished, they gave it to the school library.

What will you do with your Caring Book when it is finished?

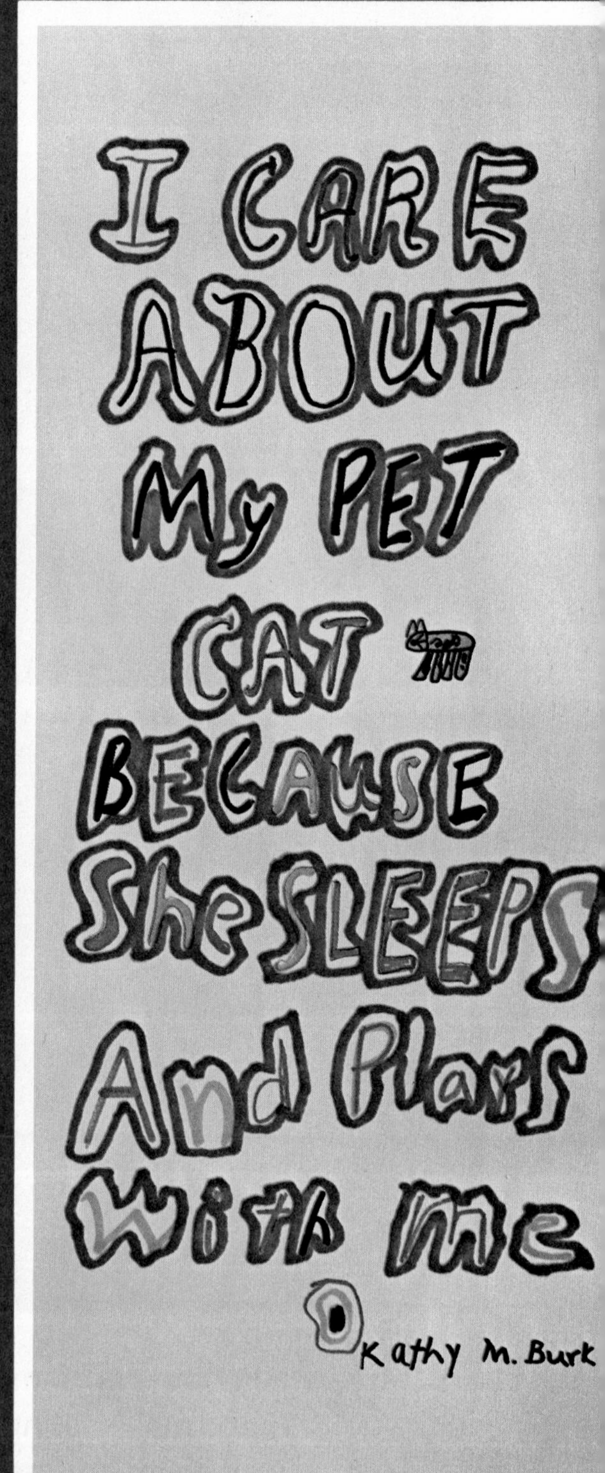

People should not litter.
trash can

I CARE ABOUT My Friend IN MY Old NEIGHBOR HOOD.
P and G store
DUCK 1.57
Meat 2.69
Lame dog food 67¢
BRADLEYS
Duke cat food 67¢

Other Things to Try

Write a poem about your street. If you like, write about your town. What kind of town do you wish you lived in?

What do you do when someone is mean to you? What do you do when someone

sticks out a tongue?
calls you a bad name?
grabs something away from you?

Act out what you would do. Suppose you want to change the mean person's way of behaving. Act out what you would do then.

Self Study

1. Why do you think some people are mean? Who is the kindest person you know? How do you think that person became so kind?

2. How do you feel when you are working? Next time you feel sad, make something beautiful. See how you feel then.

WE CARE

My father is helping me with Rusty. He loves horses, too. We live on a small ranch in Kansas. Dad says an animal will always know if you love him. I hope Rusty knows.

My dad is teaching me to play the accordion. He is a very good teacher. I want to do well. Daddy loves music even more than I do. I hope the sounds I make don't hurt his ears.

I'm showing my father some stories I have written. Some day I hope Mom and Dad will be proud of me. Maybe I'll be a great writer! They say they are proud of me now.

We went into the store. I told this man how much I liked the things there. He said there is an art center near his store! I could take lessons there. I hope Mom will let me.

Here I am with my grandfather. He is my best friend. He can make anybody laugh. He rides a bicycle on the high wire. We go all over the country. Every year we go to Florida.

Here is my whole family. We are at a park in California. I am showing my big brother what I've learned. He never had dancing in school. My little brother is watching. My mom and dad like to know what we learn in school.

CARING
FOR
BEAUTY

Listen to the wind.
Feel the soft rain.
Watch a bird fly.
Smell a pretty flower.
Taste a snowflake.

There are so many beautiful things to see and hear. There is so much beauty to smell, and taste, and touch. What do you like most about the world? How will you help take care of the beautiful things in the world?

What Do You Like?

What seems most beautiful to you?

Is it sand and sun?
Is it a big hug?
Is it a new sled?
Is it someone you know?

Find a way to share what seems beautiful to you. You might want to describe it. Maybe you will bring a picture of it to class.

Now see and hear what other boys and girls chose. How many different beautiful things were chosen? How many of them were made by people? How many of them are found in *nature* (NAY·chur)? How many are people or animals?

Nature is everything in the world except the things that people have made.

What songs tell about beauty? How else can you tell about beautiful things? For one idea, please turn the page.

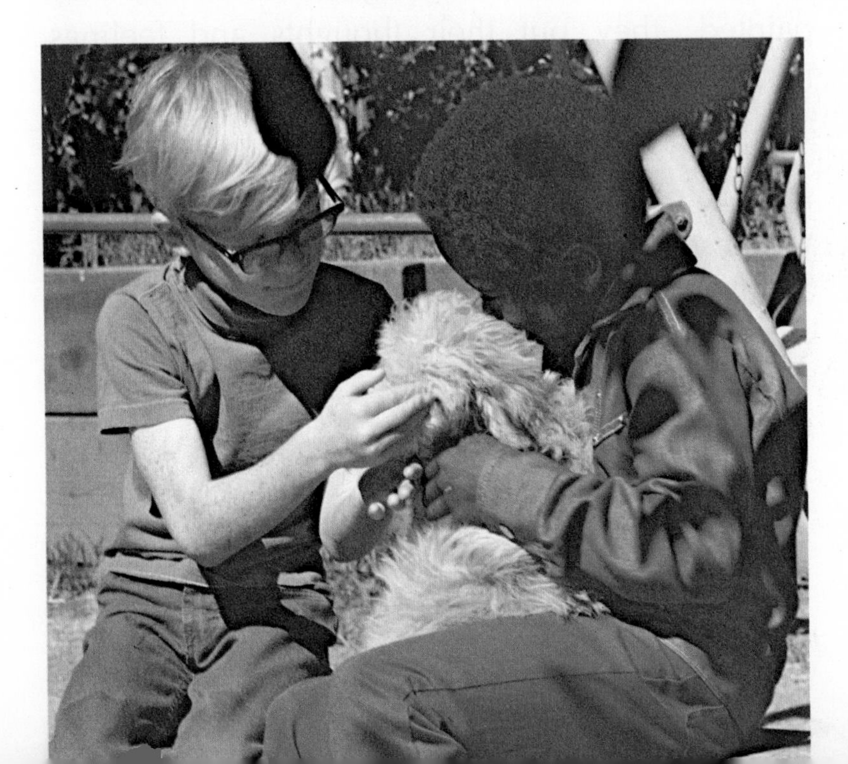

Pictures of Nature

There are so many beautiful things in nature. Painting pictures of nature is one way of telling about it. These pictures are *landscapes*.

Chinese artists painted these landscapes many years ago. Two of the landscapes are on *scrolls* (SKROLS). The artists painted on long strips of paper. Then the strips were rolled up. When people looked at these paintings, they unrolled the scrolls slowly. They looked carefully at each part of the picture. How does looking carefully help you see beauty?

Look carefully at the landscapes. How are these mountains and trees different from the ones you have seen?

Before Chinese artists painted landscapes, they visited a place many times. Then they thought about it for a long while. When they painted, they put their thoughts and feelings in their pictures.

Did the Chinese artists use loud colors or soft colors? See how small the houses look. What can you tell about how the artists felt about mountains? How do their paintings make you feel about mountains?

The landscapes on page 65 were done by Chiang Ts'an (JI·AHN SAHN) (top), Ch'iu Ying (CHIW YIN) (right), and Li Ch'eng (LEE CHAN) (left). Li Ch'eng's landscape is more than a thousand years old.

Artists in the United States did these paintings. Which one might be called a *seascape?* Which painting do you like best?

How do you think the artists felt about what they saw? How did they seem to feel about people and nature?

The artists are Grandma Moses (this page), Winslow Homer (top, page 67), Dong Kingman (bottom, page 67).

Artists use colors and lines to show feelings. What feelings might you show with red, jagged lines? Now, move to show red, jagged lines. What might you show with blue, flowing lines? Move in a way that shows blue, flowing lines.

What kinds of lines do you see in each painting? What kinds of colors do you see? How do the lines and colors make you feel?

KINGMAN

People your age painted these pictures. Where do you think they live? How do they feel about the things they see around them? Are these places you would like to visit?

What colors did each artist use? What different kinds of lines can you find in these paintings? How does each picture make you feel?

SELF EXPRESSION

You can tell about your world, too. Go for a walk near your home. Look around you. What do you see that is far away? What do you see that is near? Draw some of these things.

Look for colors that you like. Listen for sounds. Make notes about them. How do the things that you see and hear make you feel?

Touch some of the things you see. Lay your hand on a brick wall. Feel the trunk of a tree. Is the bark smooth or rough?

Now, make a painting about your walk. Look at your notes. What will make a good picture?

Think about how your walk made you feel. What kind of lines will you use? Do you feel like using bright or quiet colors?

You may want to make a scroll. Your scroll might show your walk from beginning to end. What will you show? Are there some things you will leave out?

Adam L

Other Things to Try

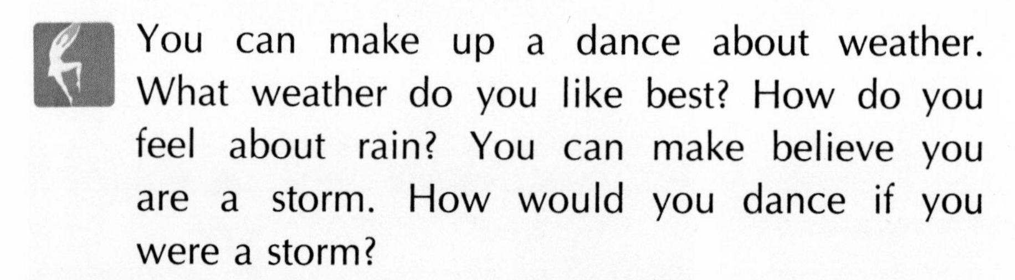

You can make up a dance about weather. What weather do you like best? How do you feel about rain? You can make believe you are a storm. How would you dance if you were a storm?

Find some songs that tell about nature. It will be easy to find words that tell about nature. Can you find *melodies,* too? How would rain music sound? How would sun music sound? Can you make up some music about nature? What music instrument will you use?

Do you remember what *melodies* are? Please see page 47 if you do not.

Self Study

1 What do you see when you look at clouds? Do all people see the same thing? How do you know? How would you tell about clouds? Why don't all people tell about clouds in the same way?

2 Which painting in this book do you like best? Suppose you could put that painting on the classroom wall. What color would you use for the background? What kind of frame would you put around it? Can you tell why?

Each person is beautiful in a different way.
What will be your way?

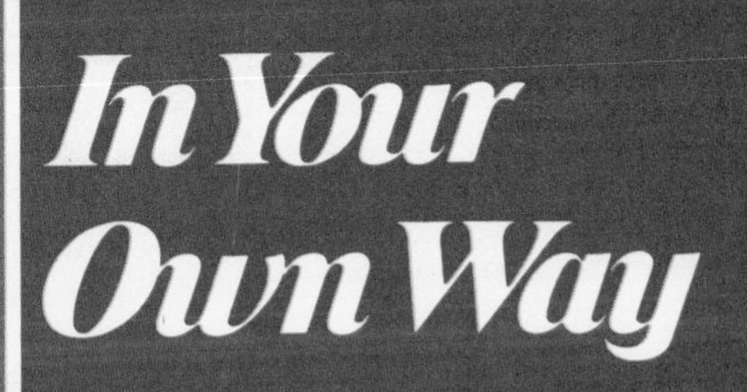

In Your Own Way

What feels beautiful when you wear it? It may be a sweater. It may be a pair of shoes. Some things seem beautiful to you just because you love them.

Many plain things are beautiful. You like them just as they are. You may really like their shape or color.

Fancy things may be beautiful, too. They may have bright colors or pretty designs. They may be decorated in a beautiful way.

Many people like to gather beautiful things. The children in these pictures have started *collections*. What is each child *collecting*?

Christopher Tavares goes to school in Massachusetts. On the next page is a list of the things he gathered.

a little stone that shines in the sun

some wheels from an old clock

a piece of brick, because he likes that shade of red

a dried flower that has a sweet smell

a piece of velvet, beautiful to touch

Chris decided to put all of his things together. He had found a piece of wood at the beach. He liked the colors and lines he saw in the wood. He thought the wood would be a good background for his collection. He arranged his things on the wood. Then he pasted them down.

Perhaps you will start a collection this year. What things can you find for your collection?

Telling About Beauty

Some people gather and keep beautiful things. Others paint beautiful pictures. You can tell about beauty in many ways.

What beautiful things do you see and hear around you? What people do you know who have beauty in them?

Perhaps you will write a poem about beauty. Each person will have something different to write about. Each person will tell about beauty in his or her own special way.

E-Yeh-Shure' (ee·YAH·shoo) is a Pueblo (PWEB·loh) Indian girl. She wrote this poem when she was 15. Do you remember what *chanting* means? *In earnest* means seriously.

Beauty is seen
In the sunlight,
The trees, the birds,
Corn growing and people working
Or dancing for their harvest.

Beauty is heard
In the night,
Wind sighing, rain falling,
Or a singer *chanting*
Anything *in earnest*.

Beauty is in yourself,
Good deeds, happy thoughts
That repeat themselves
In your dreams,
In your work,
And even in your rest.

Yaqui Deer Dance

This Yaqui (YAH·kee) Indian of Mexico is dancing the deer dance. When a Yaqui does this dance, he is telling about what his people believe. The Yaquis believe that deer are brave animals. They believe that deer allow the Yaquis to hunt them for food.

The Yaquis feel grateful to the deer. That is why they made up the deer dance. The dance tells how deer live and die for others.

What animals are you grateful for? How do you show how you feel about them?

Imitates means copies. A person who imitates something tries to look or act like it.

The Yaqui deer dancer *imitates* (IM·uh·tayts) the way the deer moves. He tries to show how the deer feels.

You can show feelings in a dance. First, try to show how a deer might listen. Use your whole body. Suppose the deer heard a noise. How will you show that?

Show different feelings as you move. See if others can tell what you are showing.

All over the world people dance. The pictures on this page show some of the many different ways people dance.

You can do dances that people have made up. You can make up your own dances. What dances do you like to do?

Special Gifts

People have different ideas about what is beautiful. Sometimes it seems hard to choose a gift for someone you love. You worry, "Will she like this color? Maybe she likes plain things. Suppose she won't like so many colors!"

Almost everyone likes to receive things that people they love have made. Why do you think that is so?

What kind of gift do you like to get? What kind of gift do you like to give? Have you ever received a gift of something living? Sharing is a way of giving.

People make beautiful things to keep. They make beautiful things to give away, too.

The Lakota (luh·KOH·tuh) Indians of South Dakota give things as a sign of thanks. A "giveaway" is often an important part of their *celebrations* (sel·uh·BRAY·shuns).

Celebrations are times when people show that they are very happy.

The pictures on this page were taken at a Lakota giveaway. A family is celebrating the adoption of a child.

SELF EXPRESSION

IN THE NORTHWEST

In McCleary, Washington, a class had a giveaway. The gifts were things the boys and girls had made. They gave presents to their parents and to school helpers. Some of the gifts were songs and dances.

Perhaps your class could have a giveaway, too. The gifts might be things you have made this year. Who will receive your gifts? How will you decide?

If you are going to have dances, perhaps one group can plan them. Will you also need a group to plan for music?

What kinds of beautiful things will you give away? Whom will you invite to your giveaway? How will you invite them?

OFFICERS

Other Things to Try

Make up a short play about *receiving* the best gift you can think of. Then make up a play about *giving* the best gift you can think of.

Make something that people will take in with their eyes. Make something that will remind people of one of these things.

a cold, windy day	a party
a bad dream	an old, old lady

Will you use paint? Will you use clay? What other ways can you think of?

Self Study

1 Suppose you met someone who was just like you. Suppose he or she looked like you. Suppose this person talked like you and thought like you. What would you do? What would you say to that person?

2 Look at the clothes you are wearing. What is plain? What is decorated with many different lines and colors? When do you like to wear clothes that are plain? Which seems most beautiful to you—plain or decorated things?

Suppose you were in each picture.
What sounds would you hear?
What sounds do you like best?

Making Melodies

Listen very quietly to the sounds *inside* you. Can you hear the sound of your own breathing? What does your breathing sound like?

Now listen to the sounds *around* you. You may hear the sound of voices. You may hear a dog barking. You may hear wind and rain at the window. hat are these sounds like?

Are they like this?

Are they more like this?

What's the loudest sound you ever remember hearing? What's the softest sound you ever remember hearing? What sounds would you like to turn off?

Noise is made up of sounds. Music is made up of sounds. What is the difference between noise and music?

Here is a way to show the difference. Make some noise for thirty seconds. Then make up thirty seconds of music. You may use your voice. You may use anything that makes sounds. Now can you tell someone else how music and noise are different?

Making Music

Patterns are repeated sounds, colors, or actions. Can you tell which is the pattern on page 87?

You have just made up some music. Someone who makes up music is called a *composer* (kum·POH·zur). Composers listen carefully to sounds. They remember sounds they have heard. They put interesting sounds together in different *patterns*.

All over the world, people make up music. These are some of the many different ways music can sound.

LOUD and SOFT

FAST and SLOW

LONG and SHORT

Can you find these sounds in the music you made up? Try making these sounds in different patterns.

People all over the world sing and play music. Suppose you were in each picture on the next page. What sounds would you be hearing? What might you be learning?

People often write down sounds. Why do you think they do that? There are many ways to write down sounds.

Here is one way people used to write down sounds in China.

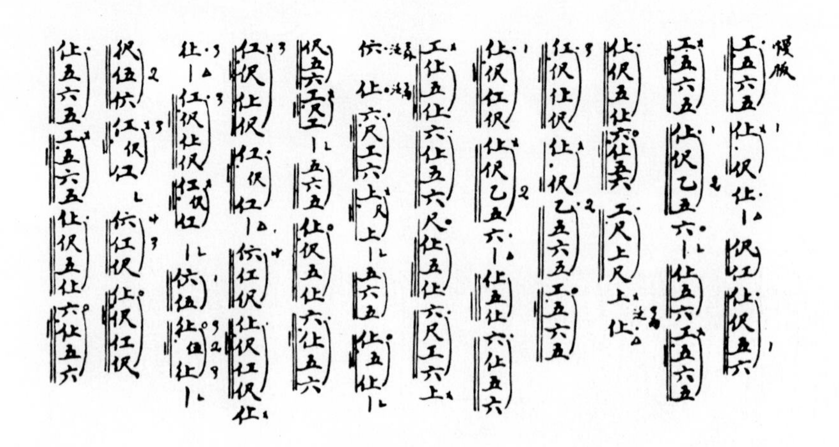

Here is one way composers used to write down sounds in Europe.

Some children your age wrote down sounds like this.

In your music book, sounds are written on lines and spaces. This group of sounds is called the *C major scale*.

You can play the C major scale on many music instruments. The letters show you where to find the notes. The instrument at the top is a xylophone (ZIY·luh·fohn). You may already know how to find the C major scale on a piano.

See if you can sing or play this song.

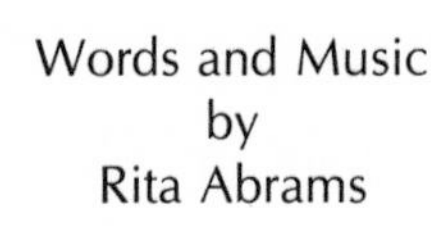

Words and Music
by
Rita Abrams

As you sing Rita's song, move your hand in the air. Show how the music goes up or down. Show when the music stays the same.

Point to the longest notes. Which notes are shortest? Where do the notes skip spaces and lines?

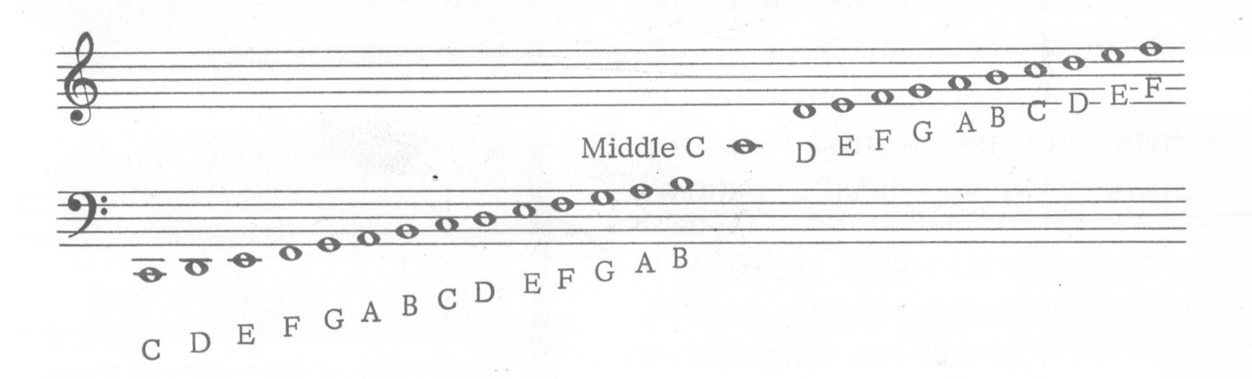

Look carefully at this chart. It is the *Grand Staff*. The Grand Staff was used in Europe more than 500 years ago. People today still use the Grand Staff as a way of writing down sounds. Can you find the notes from Rita's song on this *staff*?

A *staff* is the lines and spaces on which music is written.

SELF EXPRESSION

You, too, can write a song. Perhaps you will write new words to Rita's melody. Perhaps you will make up a new melody and new words.

You might want to write about what you would see from the top of a tree. Say your words four or five times. Listen to the rhythm of the words. Clap the rhythm. Do you hear a pattern?

Now think about how you will show your rhythm pattern. Perhaps you will use long dashes to show strong beats. How will you show weaker beats?

Choose two or three notes that you like to hear. Perhaps you will draw a line to show how the notes go up and down. You might want to write your notes on a staff. You might want to make up your own way of writing down sounds.

If you have a music instrument, play and sing your song for someone. Then see if your friends can sing your song.

I'm swaying in the
Of the tallest tree and
Singing about
that I see.
Animals Animals
all around me.
Kathy

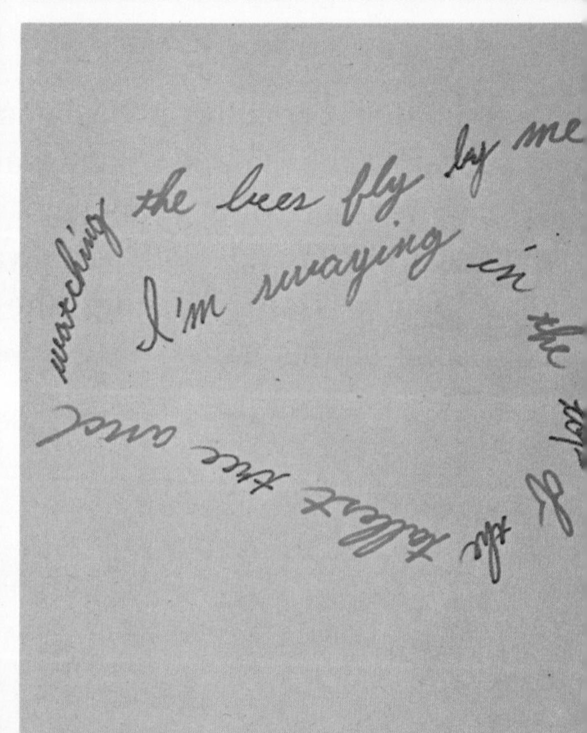

START HERE

SWAYING AT THE TOP OF THE TREE SWAYING SWAYING

CHARLENE

START HERE

Monkeys Monkeys are smiling at me!

I'm swaying in the top of the tallest tree and the tree is taller than me.

Richard

Other Things to Try

Would you like to make up a secret message? You may use numbers or other signs as *symbols* (SIM·buls) for letters. Send a secret message to a friend. How will the friend be able to read your symbols? Clue: Tell him patterns will help!

Symbols are marks or signs that stand for other things. A $ is a symbol for money.

Every time you move, you use space, time, and energy in different ways. A dance is made up of many ways of moving. How does a dancer remember all of them? Make up your own way of writing down a dance. Begin with just three or four moves. How will you write them down? Will you use words or symbols?

Self Study

1 You have learned that music has a pattern. Does your day have a pattern? Does your week have a pattern? Suppose your day had no pattern. How do you think you would like that? How can you change patterns in your life that you don't like?

2 People write down music so they won't forget it. Who will never forget you? How would you like to be remembered? What or whom will you never forget?

How will you add to the beauty in the world?

Making Things Beautiful

People buy beautiful things in a store. They like to make beautiful things, too. Many people like to make things by hand.

Find something made by a person you know. If you can, bring it in. Share it with the class. Is it too big to bring in? You could draw a picture that tells about it.

Materials are what something is made of.

Run your fingers over each thing made by hand. Pick it up. Touch it all over. What *materials* (muh·TIR·ee·uls) were used in each one? Is there something made of clay? Is there something made of yarn? Is the yarn cotton or wool? How can you tell?

Most things are made of more than one kind of material. What materials do you like to see and feel together?

Write the name of each material on a small card like this.

WOOD	COTTON	GLASS

Now get together with three other children. Talk about the materials. Which seemed heaviest? Which seemed softest? Which seemed strongest? Which seemed smoothest? Put the cards in this order.

Heaviest to Lightest
Hardest to Softest
Strongest to Weakest
Roughest to Smoothest

Will the same materials always be first or last? Does everyone agree on where the cards should go? What happens when you don't agree?

Clay and Cloth

All over the world people make pots. They weave cloth, too.

The Kpelle (PE·luh) people of Liberia in Africa use clay pots for cooking. They store water and grain in big clay jars. The top row of pictures shows one way to make a pot.

Why do you think the woman is decorating her bowl? Suppose you could *hear* this pattern. How do you think it would sound? Choose two or three tones on an instrument. Choose a tone for each part of the pattern. Can you play the pattern on an instrument?

After the pots have been decorated, they are put into a very hot fire. Fire makes clay hard. Clay stays hard after it is cool.

Among the Kpelle, weaving is done by the men. The bottom row of pictures shows how weaving is done.

First, the women spin thread from cotton. Then they color the thread. The men take the thread and weave strips of cloth. Some of the patterns are very simple. Others are decorated with animals and flowers.

Have you ever tried to weave anything? Perhaps you will try weaving paper or yarn.

Please find Liberia on a map.

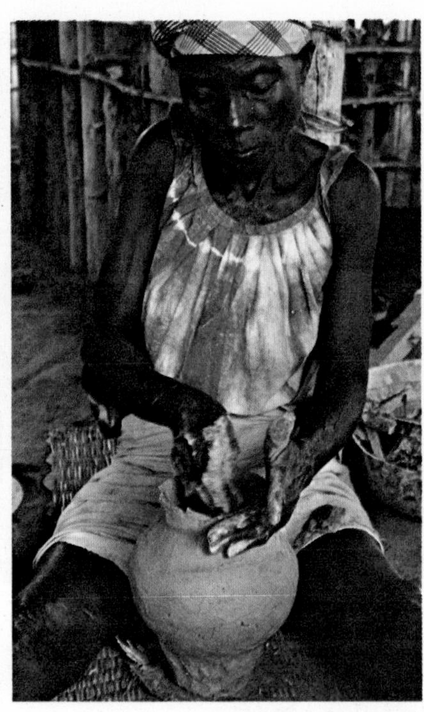

All Kinds of Houses

People like to have beauty all around them. They make everyday things beautiful.

Some houses are very small and simply made. Some houses are large. Many families may live in an apartment house. People live in cabins and in castles.

What makes a house beautiful to you? Which of these houses would you like to live in?

Houses are made of different shapes and forms. What shapes and forms can you find in these houses?

Houses are made of different materials. Can you tell what these houses are made of?

Houses are of many different colors. Sometimes the color is the color of the material used. Sometimes houses are painted. What colors do you like for houses?

Different houses look well in different places. Look at the houses on this page. Where would you put them in the pictures on page 105?

Does everyone agree about where the houses should go? Which house do you like best? Why do you like it?

SELF EXPRESSION

Suppose your family needs a place to live. You may choose a house or an apartment. You may choose to build a new house. Perhaps you like older houses.

Suppose you could live anywhere you wanted. Would you stay where you are? Would you move to a different town? Find some places that sound interesting. See what you can find out about them.

Next, think about what people in your family like to do. What kind of home would be most useful to them?

Some people your age drew these houses. You may want to draw a picture of the house you would like. Will you draw a real house or a dream house?

Show what materials you would use in your house. What colors would make your house beautiful?

First, draw the outside. Perhaps you will use another sheet of paper to show the inside.

Brick
Brick
Silk
Silk
Silk
Brick
wood
Brick

Other Things to Try

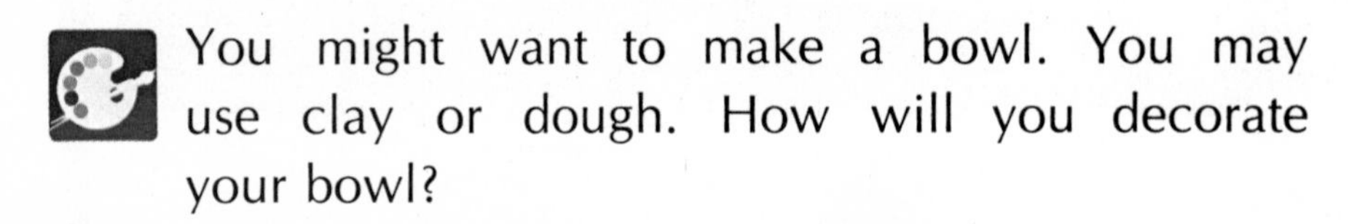

You might want to make a bowl. You may use clay or dough. How will you decorate your bowl?

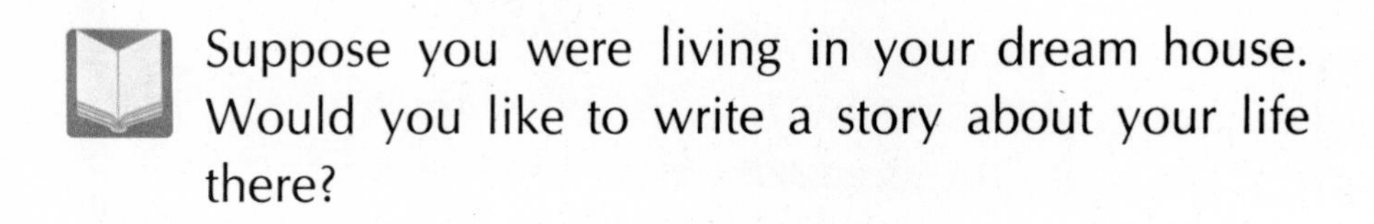

Suppose you were living in your dream house. Would you like to write a story about your life there?

Self Study

1. Why do you think people make things at home? Do you think things made by hand are worth the time they take to make?
2. Suppose you knew how to make anything you chose. What would you choose to make? What would you choose to buy at the store?
3. Find something useful that could be made more beautiful. How would you change it, if you could?

WE LIKE

I am zooming through this tunnel. I like fast music best. Sometimes we make up dances. I like to do that, too. My teacher says dancing takes *skill*. You get skill when you try something over and over. If you like it, you get better and better.

I am watching Mary make a pot. She is really good at it. The pot takes shape slowly. I love the way clay feels and smells. Mom says I can be in this art class!

Here are some pictures I took. That's me in the middle. I like to take pictures around my town. It is in New Mexico.

I wish I could spend all my time with horses. Rusty is so smart. He knows when I am feeling bad. He always makes me feel good again. He needs me to feed him. I keep him clean, too.

This is my dad, his dad, and me. They are showing me how to walk funny. They say I have a gift for clowning. I hope so!

Dad says I am getting better at the accordion. I am playing for my aunt and her kids. He helps me if I forget. After I played the songs I knew, everybody clapped!

CARING FOR DIFFERENT VIEWS

An astronaut looks at the sky and asks questions. A painter looks at the sky and asks questions.

People search for truth in many different ways. Sometimes they find different answers to their questions.

What questions do you ask?

Where will you search to find answers?

How Do You Know?

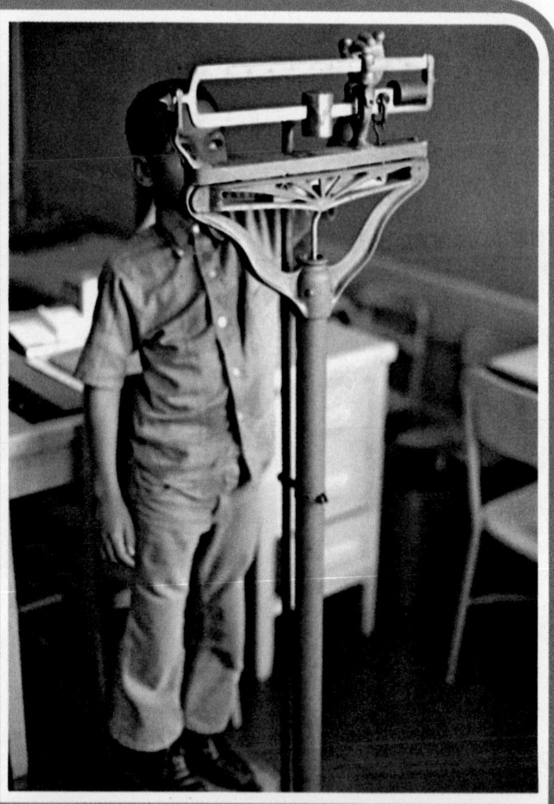

How does a scientist find out truth? Here is one way.

Look carefully at these lines.

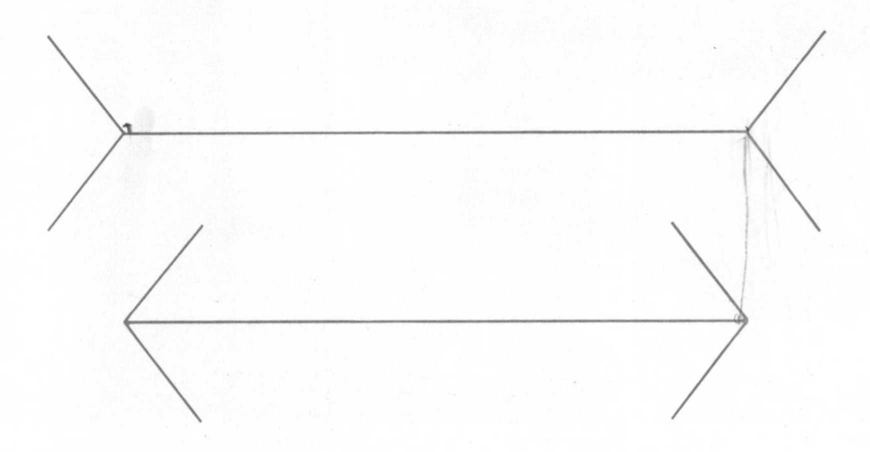

Which line is longer? How can you prove that your answer is true?

Richie and Donald are twins. Richie says he is taller than Donald. Donald says he is taller than Richie. They have many fights about this.

Suppose you were a judge. How would you decide this case? What tool might you use to help you decide?

Sometimes it's easy to find out truth. Sometimes it isn't easy at all. When isn't it easy? You can find that out for yourself.

Ask a friend to gather some little things. Ask your friend to put them in a box. Cover your eyes. Take the things out of the box. Tell what each one is. How can you tell what your friend has gathered?

You may be quite sure about some things. You may be not at all sure about others. Are you really sure of any of the things?

Suppose your friend tries to trick you. Have you ever been fooled by your senses? When can you count on your senses? You can't count on your senses all the time. What, then, can you count on?

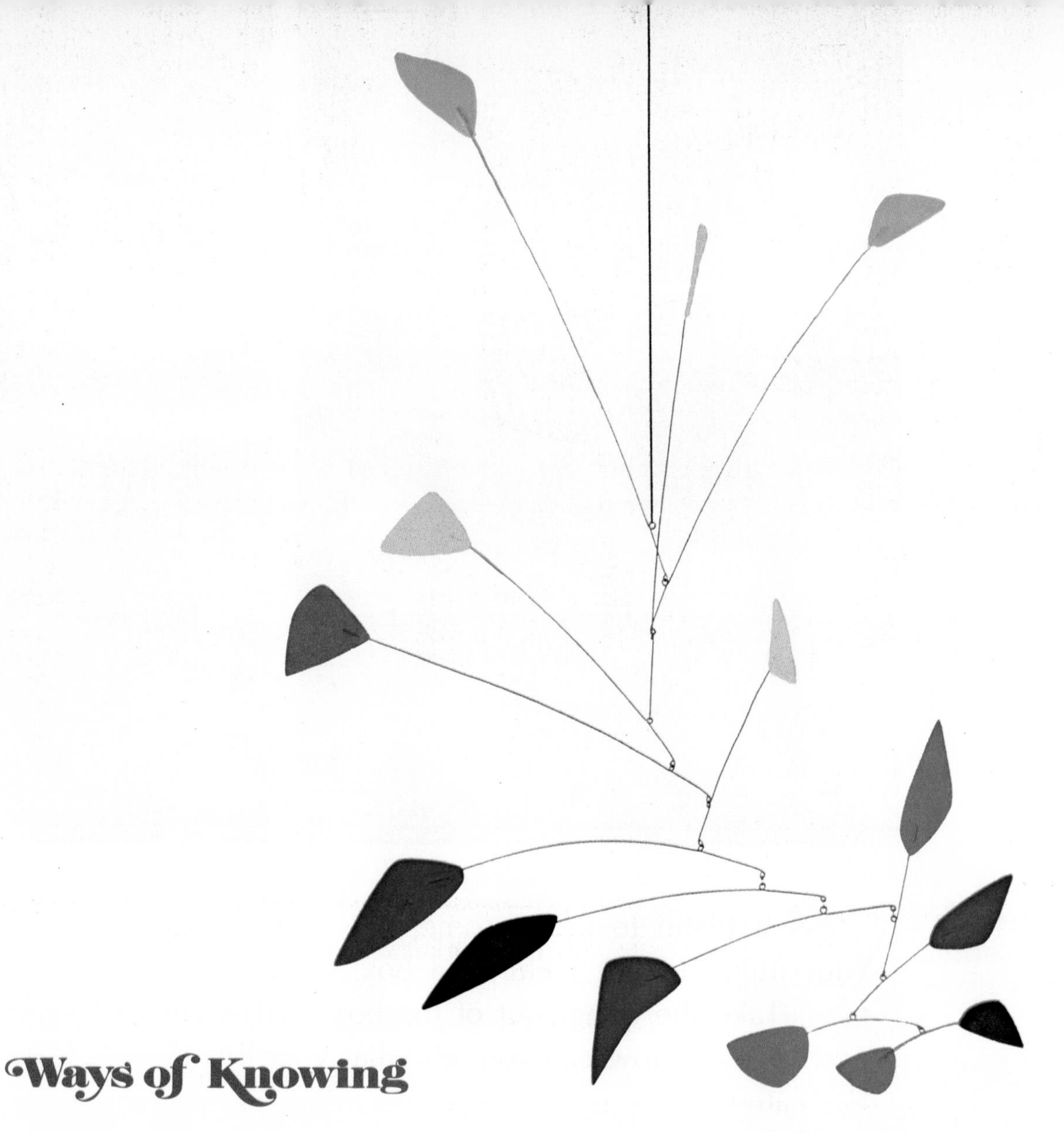

Ways of Knowing

Frank likes to go to art and science *museums* (myoo·ZEE·ums). One day he went to an art museum. He saw this mobile (MOH·beel). Have you ever seen a mobile? This one was made by Alexander Calder (CALL·der).

Museums are places for keeping and showing works of art and nature.

Frank saw the mobile move around and around. He wondered how it moved. Finally, he thought he knew. He said to himself "I'm going to make one of those." You can see him making his mobile on the next page.

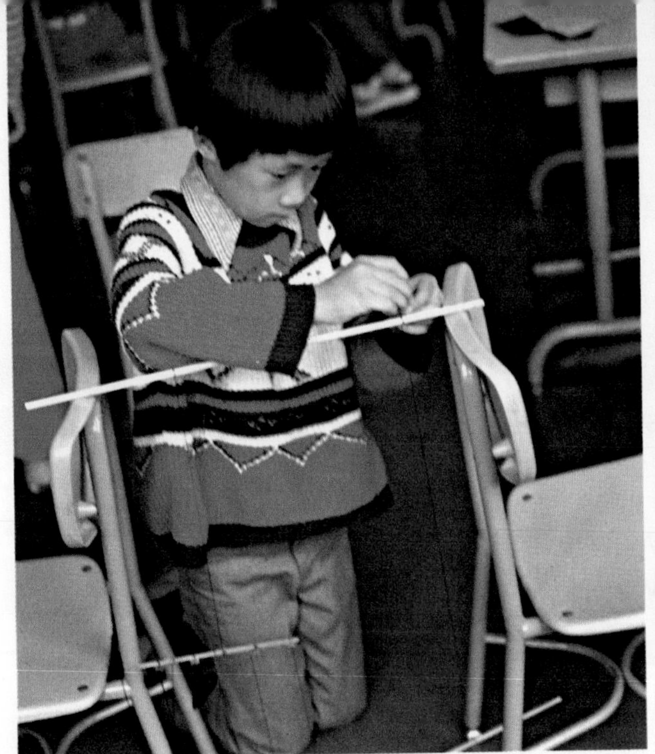

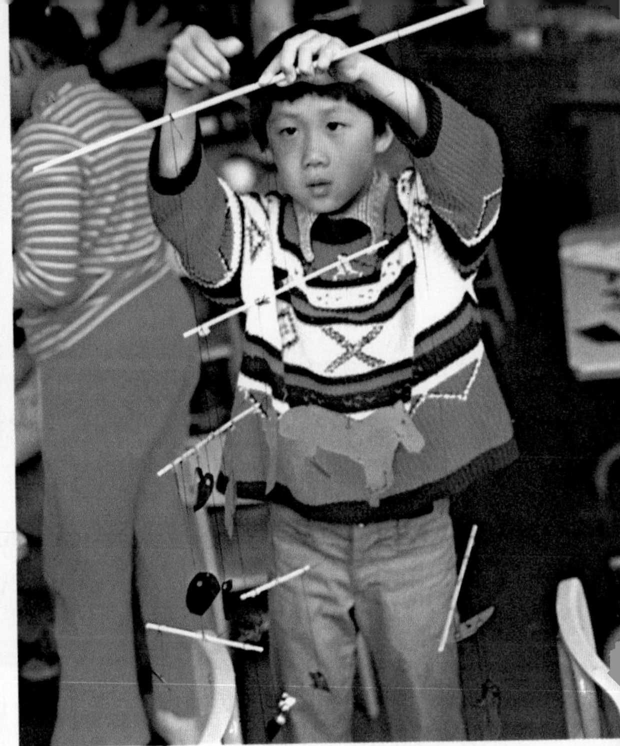

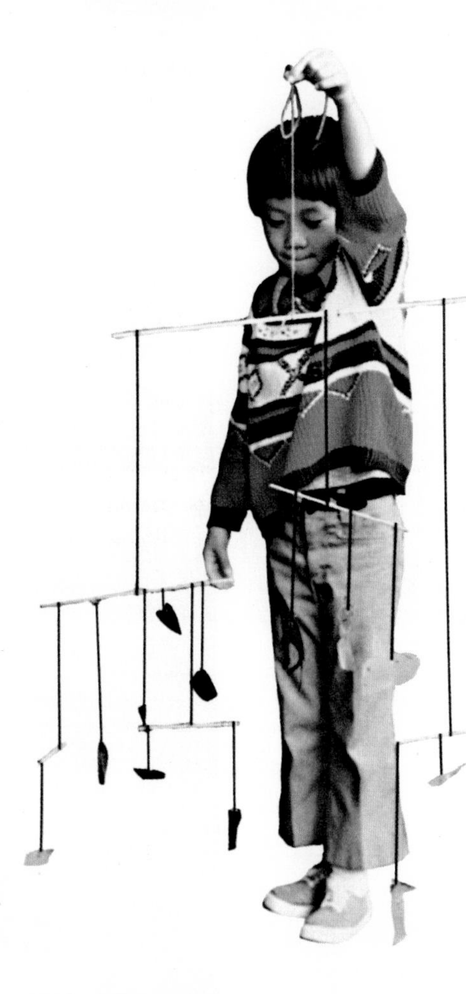

Frank wondered about the mobile. He asked, "How does it work?"

He planned it.
He made it.
He saw it work.
He found the answer to his question.

You, too, can find out about something by trying it. You may have an idea for a new kind of kite. You may have an idea for a new way to train your dog.

People are always having new ideas. How can they find out if their ideas are good ones? You can try out other people's ideas. You can try out your own ideas. That is one very good way to find out truth.

Men and women today may choose to be barbers or bankers, artists or carpenters, conductors or lawyers, engineers or jockeys.

Look again at the words in color. Does everyone agree on what these words mean? Suppose people don't agree.

You might go to a dictionary. You might ask your teacher. You would want to go to someone who would know.

You would want to go to an *authority* (uh·THOR·uh·tee). An authority is someone who knows a great deal about a subject. One person might be an authority on country music. Another person might be an authority on bees.

An authority doesn't know everything about everything. No one knows everything. An authority has worked long and hard on knowing one thing very well.

Who wrote your dictionary? How did your teacher become a teacher?

You can find out some things for yourself. Can you find out everything on your own? What must you count on?

The children in these pictures are counting on authorities. How are the authorities helping?

You count on others to tell the truth. How must others count on you?

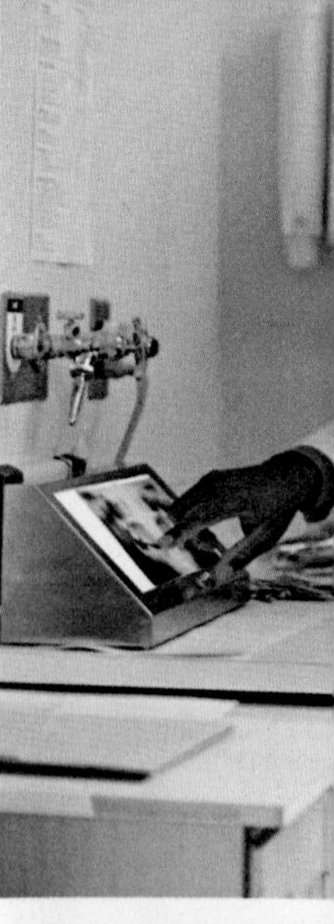

Truth and the Aztecs

Truth is important to just about everyone.

People look for truth in different places. Where they look for truth depends on what is important to them. The search for truth has gone on for a long time.

Long ago the Aztecs (AZ·teks) lived where Mexico is today. The pictures show what the Aztecs did. What were some things that were important to the Aztecs?

The stone at the top of page 123 shows other things that were important to the Aztecs. The sun is at the center of the stone. The Aztecs believed that the sun moved around the earth. Why do you suppose they thought that?

The Aztecs had two calendars. One calendar was based on the way the sun seemed to move across the sky. It divided the year into 365 days.

The other calendar was based on magic. The magic year had 260 days. The Aztecs believed that different gods ruled each hour, day, and month of the magic year.

The Aztecs used the sun calendar to help them carry on their farm work. They used the magic calendar to help them know the future.

What do these calendars tell you about the Aztecs? Was one calendar more true than the other? Why do you think so?

SELF EXPRESSION

How could someone find out what you are really like?

Here is a way to tell about you. First, find a cardboard box. Then look for pictures that tell about things you like.

You can find pictures in old magazines. Cut the pictures in any way you like.

Next, decide how you will use your pictures. Will you cover the whole box with pictures? Will you just paste pictures on top? Will you paint part of the box?

Keep adding to your box until you are happy with it. When you are happy with it, you will know you've finished your work!

Now trade boxes with someone. See how much you can tell about the other person from looking at his or her pictures.

What will you do with your box? Perhaps you will use it as a small table. Maybe you can keep things in it. You might want to just keep it to look at.

you're

Other Things to Try

On your way home from school, notice the things that feel good or bad to your senses. Make a list of these things when you get home. Maybe your list will give you an idea for a riddle! A riddle asks, "What am I?" or "What is it?"

What kind of cat can never meow? (A pussy willow or a caterpillar)

You can make up a dance about the calendar. First, decide what month you like best. How will you show the name of that month? Choose ways to move that show what you do in that month. Perhaps you will dance with other months. How will you decide who will begin?

Self Study

1. What can you find out about your calendar? Why do some months have only thirty days? Why does "leap year" happen every four years? Do people think some days are unlucky?

2. Think of three authorities that you depend on. Who else depends on these authorities? Why do you think they do or don't? How do you decide which authorities to count on?

Can the things you dream about ever come true?

About Dreams and Wishes

Two children see rain. John feels happy. He has new boots he wants to try out. Sally feels sad. Her grandfather's leg hurts when it rains.

You can use sounds to tell about feelings. Make one sound for each picture. Show how each picture makes you feel.

You can use your body to tell about feelings. Move in a way that shows how each picture makes you feel.

How do you tell about feelings with words? Jim said, "Happiness is a smile on everyone's face." Mary said, "Anger is like thunder."

What is happiness to you?
What is love to you?
What is anger to you?

Tell about each feeling with words. Maybe you'll make a picture to go with each feeling. Is each person's idea true? How can this be so?

Imagination and Truth

Imagination is the power to make up new things. Thoughts and feelings come out of your imagination. Dreams and wishes, poems and music, plays and experiments also come from your imagination. The things you dance begin there, too.

These children are doing a flying dance. You can make believe you are a bird or a plane. You can fly anywhere in your imagination. Suppose you could be anyone in the world. Suppose you could fly anywhere in a second. Whom would you choose to be? Where would you choose to go?

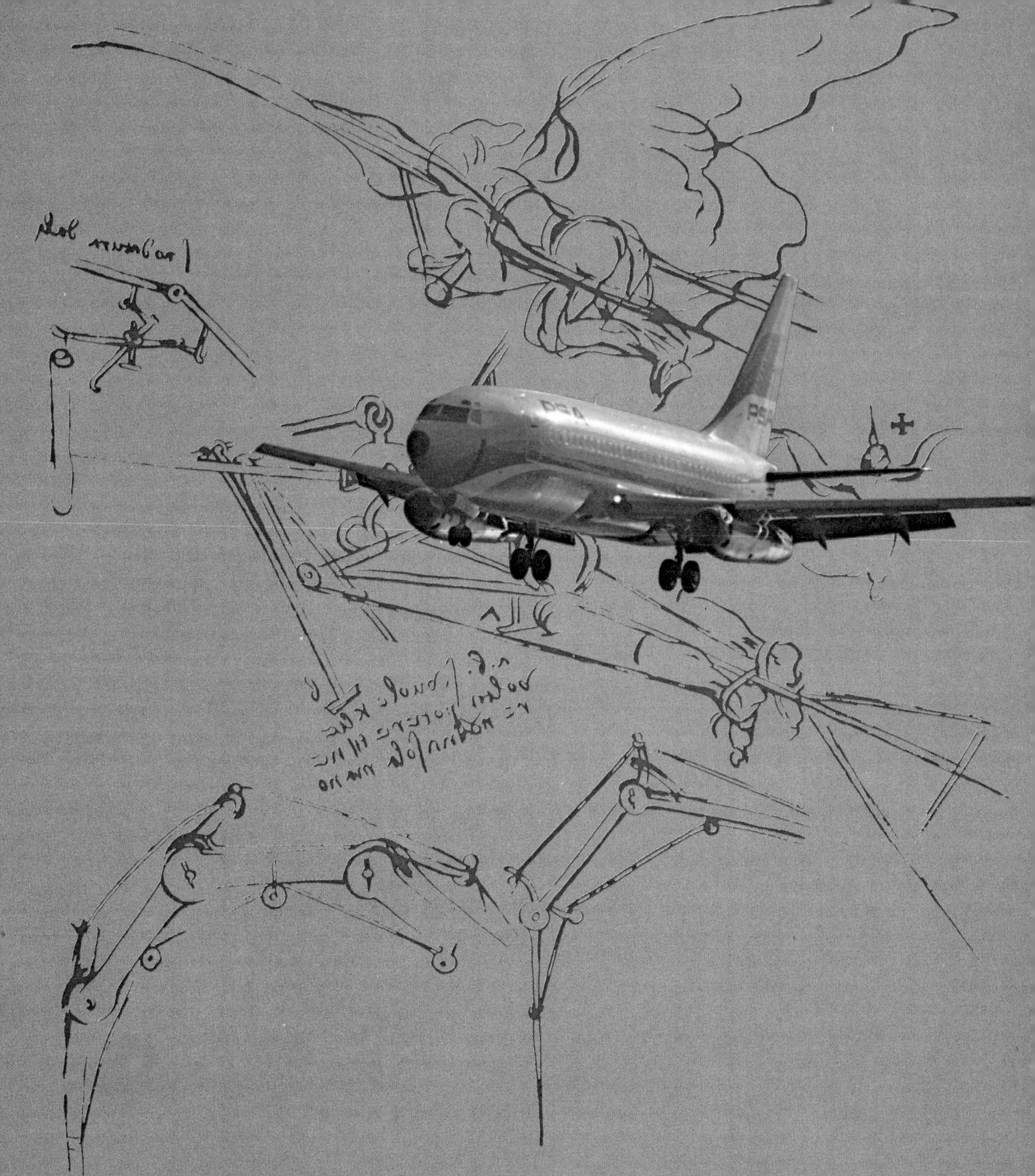

These drawings were done by Leonardo da Vinci (lay·oh·NAHR·doh duh·VIN·chee). Long ago he imagined that people might be able to fly. Many others had the same dream. How have these dreams come true?

Wish for something you really want. Close your eyes and wish hard. Do you think wishes can come true?

Have you ever wished you could eat all the candy in a candy store? Would you really want this to happen?

Think of a wish. It may be something real. It may be something funny or silly. Make up a wish poem with some other children. Here is one way you might want to do it.

Each line of the poem might begin with the words, "I wish." Each child thinks of one wish.

Some people wish for things to make life easier. They tell people what they wish. Sometimes they make their own wish happen.

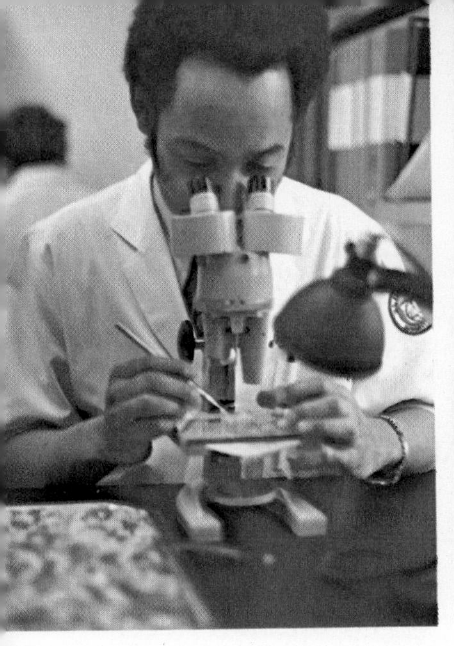

Sometimes others work to make someone's dream come true. Have any of your wishes ever come true?

How are these people working to make their dreams come true? How is each one working to find the truth or to tell the truth? Suppose you were each one of these people. How would you be adding to truth?

As you go through life you will wish for different things. Some wishes will come true. Some won't. There is plenty of time to work at making your wishes come true.

Today you might want to be a doctor. Next year you might want to be a police officer. Different things will be important to you at different times. There is plenty of time.

Stages in Life

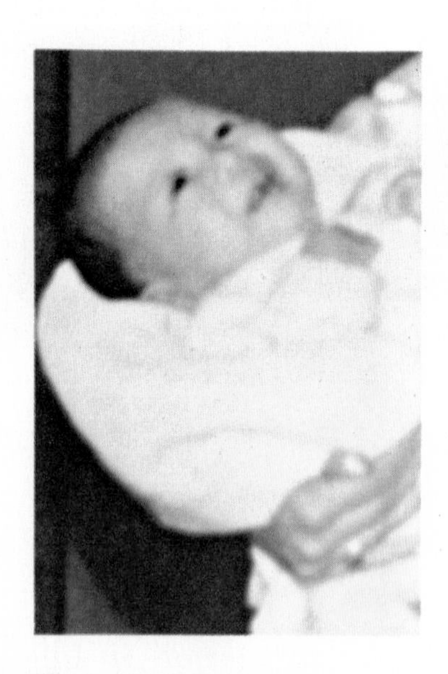

Like this boy, you go through different stages in life. Stages are like steps. You stay at each step, or stage, for a while. Then you go on to the next stage. At each stage of your life, there are new truths to learn. There are people to help you learn.

Sometimes *ceremonies* (SAYR·uh·moh·nees) happen when people go from one stage to another. A ceremony is an event done in a certain way. In a ceremony, there are rules about how things should be done.

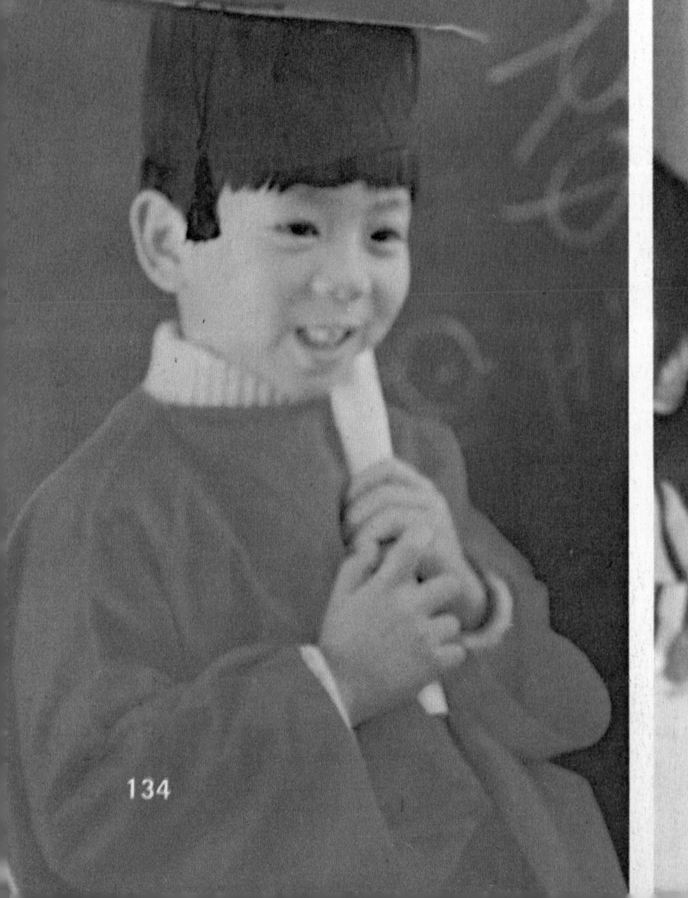

There are ceremonies for becoming a man or a woman in many parts of the world. In some places, all children of the same age take part in this ceremony.

This picture shows a ceremony in West Africa. The men are teaching the boys. They test them to see if they are brave.

Dances and music are often part of the ceremonies. The dances and music teach the children about the new lives they will have. This is one way that men and women pass on to children the truths they live by.

SELF EXPRESSION

IN THE SOUTH

A ceremony helps you go from one stage to another. It tells you about what you will find in the next stage.

A class in Nashville, Tennessee, made up a ceremony. The ceremony was for the class below it. The children told about what the next year would be like.

You can make up a ceremony for the class below yours. Here are some things you may want the class to know.

different rules
things they will study
new things they will do

Plan how you will teach these things in a ceremony.

You may want to make up a different kind of ceremony. Perhaps your ceremony will be for children who are just beginning school. Perhaps you will welcome children who have just come into your class.

Our Nature Walk
And Discoveries
NO TWO
BE ALIKE
WHEN
ABOVE EACH
LETS MEET THE LEAVES WE FOUND

We are descendants
of many countries
Netherlands

Other Things to Try

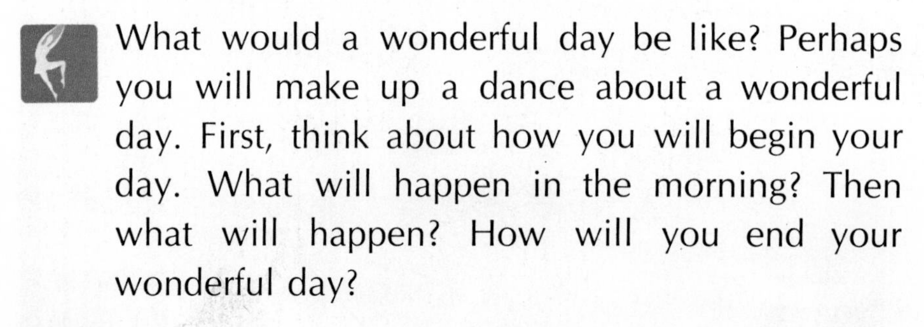

What would a wonderful day be like? Perhaps you will make up a dance about a wonderful day. First, think about how you will begin your day. What will happen in the morning? Then what will happen? How will you end your wonderful day?

Do you ever wish for something to make your life easier or more fun? Use your imagination to make an *invention* that will do it. Will it be a machine that does something better? Make a drawing of your invention. Name the parts to show how they work.

An *invention* is something that is made or done for the first time.

Self Study

1 Suppose this were a world where everyone's dreams came true. How do you think you would like that world?

2 Suppose a very young child tells you about a bad dream he had. How could you help him become less afraid? Do you ever have bad dreams? What helps you become less afraid?

What do you like to make believe?

Real and Make-Believe

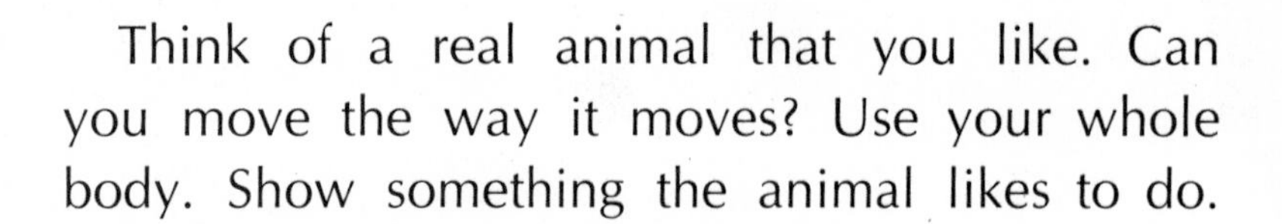

Think of a real animal that you like. Can you move the way it moves? Use your whole body. Show something the animal likes to do.

Now use your imagination. Imagine that you can change this real animal into a make-believe animal. You can make it a friendly, helpful animal. You can make it a bad, mean animal. How will you change it?

Do you have a picture of your make-believe animal in your head? Try to get as clear a picture of it as you can. Does your make-believe animal have a strange shape? What color is it?

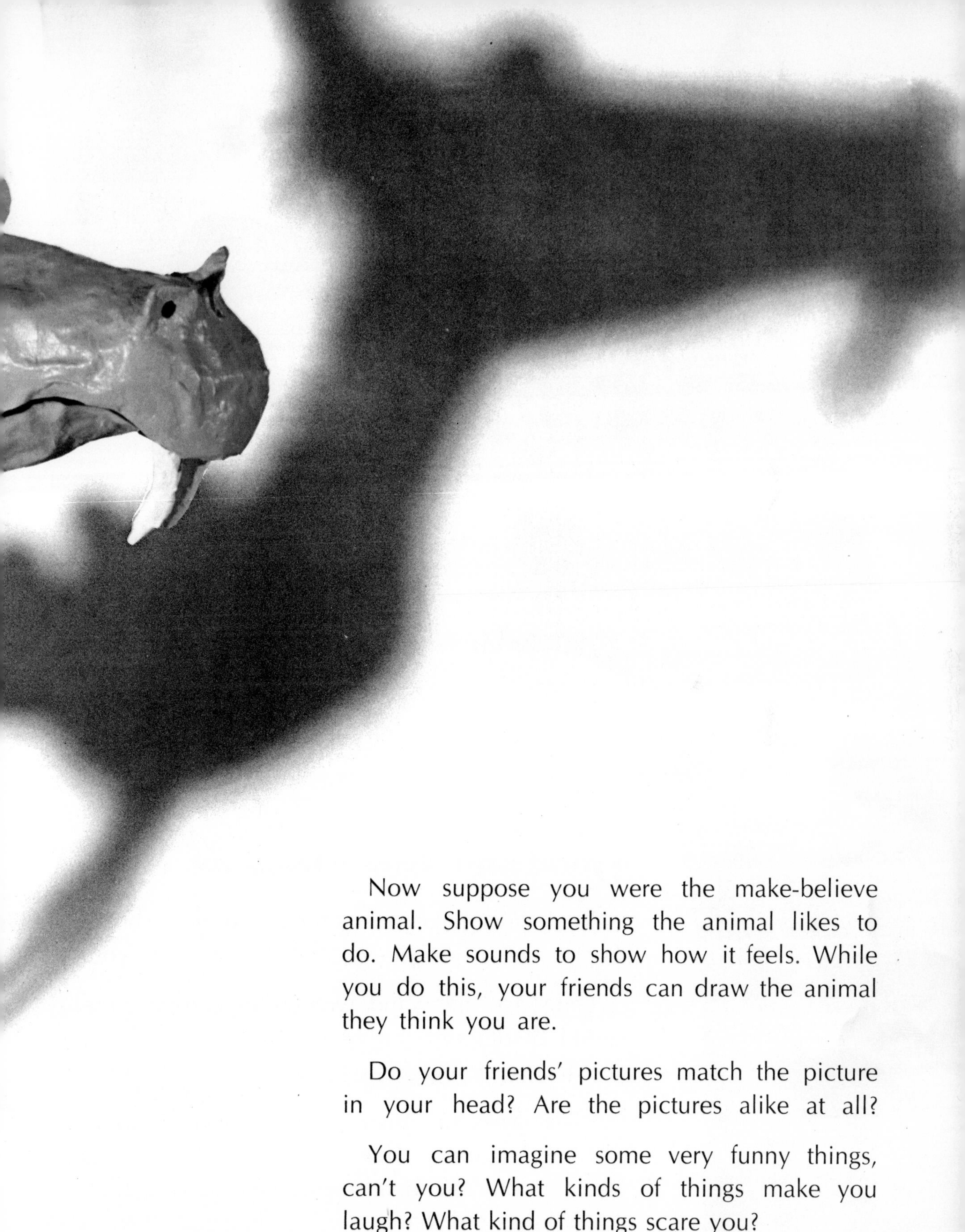

Now suppose you were the make-believe animal. Show something the animal likes to do. Make sounds to show how it feels. While you do this, your friends can draw the animal they think you are.

Do your friends' pictures match the picture in your head? Are the pictures alike at all?

You can imagine some very funny things, can't you? What kinds of things make you laugh? What kind of things scare you?

Good and Bad Dragons

You can make up animals in your head. Sometimes make-believe animals can scare you.

Long ago men and women in Europe were afraid of dragons. Brave people would go out looking for strange beasts to kill.

Long ago the Vikings (VIY·kings) lived in northern Europe. They carved dragon heads like this one on their ships. Why do you think the Vikings did that?

In China, dragons had another meaning. Long ago in China, dragons stood for forces of nature. Like wind and rain, these beasts could make good or bad things happen. The Chinese thought dragons did more good than bad.

What do you think about dragons? Are all dragons make-believe? How can you find out?

How do you think these animals move? Do they look friendly to you? What sounds do you think each animal makes?

Some of these animals are real. Some are make-believe. How will you find out which are real?

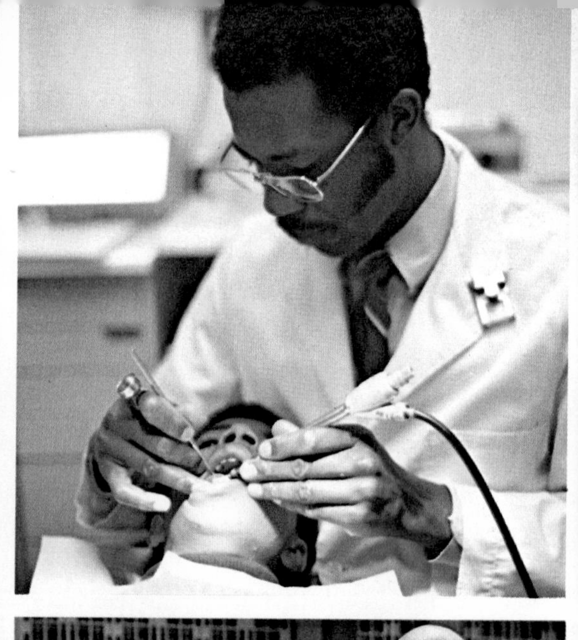

K-101

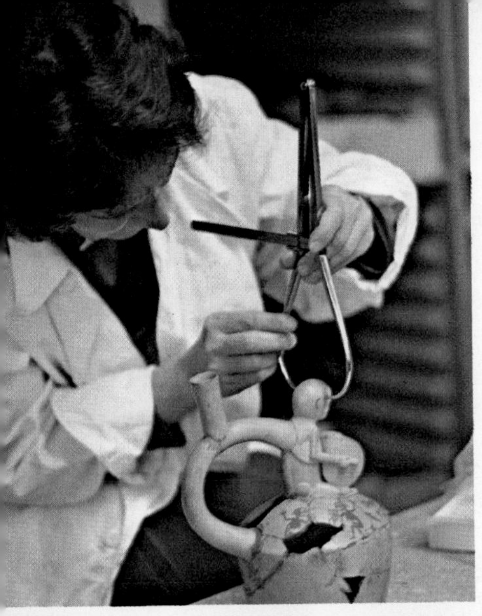

Tools and Truth

Tools help people find out what is real. They help people find out what is make-believe. What tools do you see in these pictures? What tools help people to see more and hear more?

Much has been discovered about the world. There are many secrets left. There is much for you to find out.

Some day you may use some of these tools. You can start by using your own eyes and ears. You can start by looking closely. You can start by listening carefully. You can start by caring about truth.

SELF EXPRESSION

These children wanted to find out about their turtles. They made a Truth Book about what they found out. What tools do you see in the pictures?

The children wrote about what their turtles did. They wrote about how they grew. They drew pictures of their turtles too.

Will you make a Truth Book, too? First, decide what you will study. Will it be an animal? Will it be a small piece of earth? Will it be a plant?

Find out everything you can about your subject. Watch it very closely. Take notes. What tools will you need?

Now make a record of the truth you have found. You may want some pages about make-believe in your book too. Will you write a story about how your animal talks? What other make-believe things can you imagine?

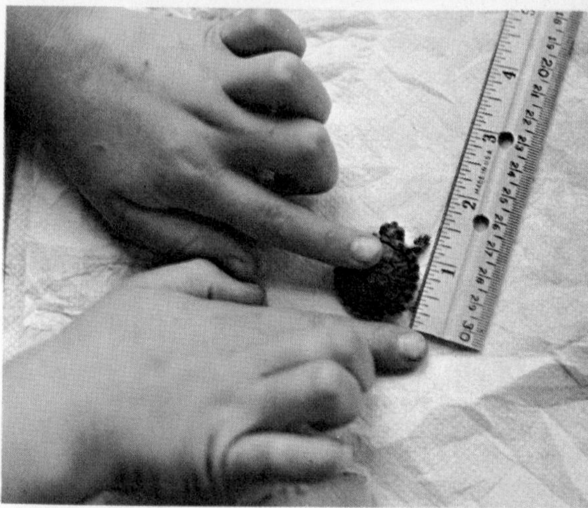

Turtle Race
Chopper
JEFFERY

Other Things to Try

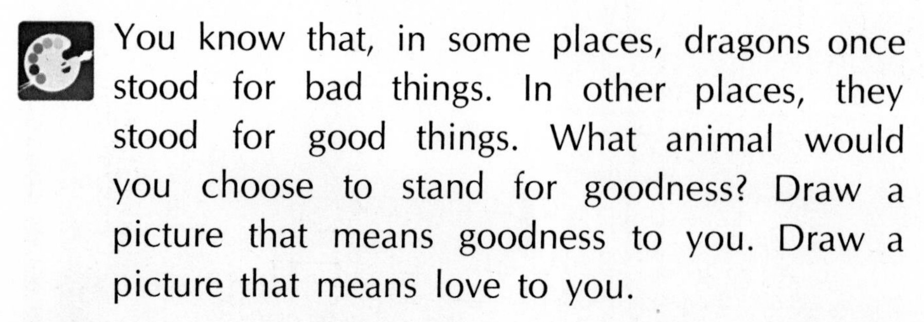

You know that, in some places, dragons once stood for bad things. In other places, they stood for good things. What animal would you choose to stand for goodness? Draw a picture that means goodness to you. Draw a picture that means love to you.

The way you move can stand for different things, too. Think of ways to move that mean these things.

I'm scared. I miss you.
I'm so happy. I like you.

Self Study

1. Are there things you used to be afraid of that you don't fear any more? How did you become less afraid?

2. Is it always easy to tell the truth? When is it easy? When is it hard?

What is being exaggerated in each picture?

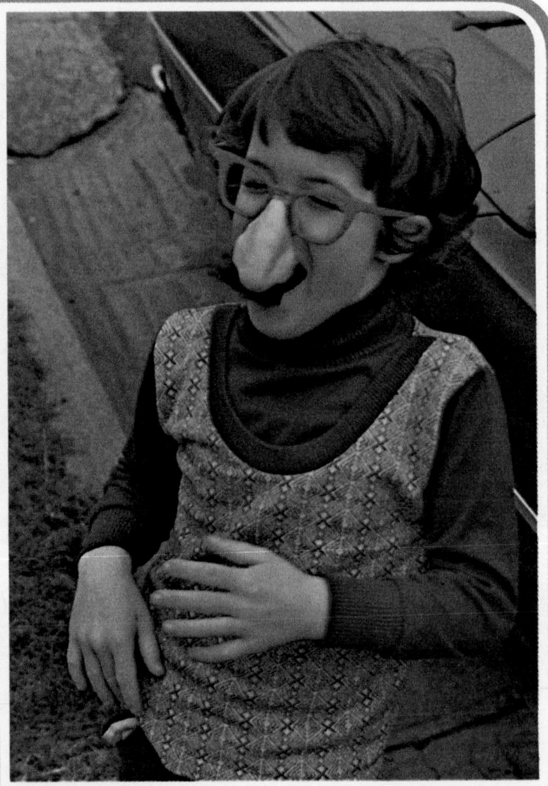

About People

How would you fill in the blank in this poem?

> Look in a mirror.
> What do you see?
> Can this ________ person
> Really be me?

Sometimes you may feel like a beautiful person. Sometimes you may feel like a funny-looking person. A mirror tells how you look on the outside. Even when you feel sad, you can smile. You can fool any mirror.

It's not so easy to fool a person. A person sees below the way you look on the outside. Here is something you can try.

Choose a friend to be your mirror. Ask your friend to do exactly what you do. Then make up five different ways to move. You might want to move high first. Then move low. Then you might want to do a turn that no one has ever seen before. Then do any kind of jump you want to do. You might end by doing something very fast or very slow. Make up your own five ways of moving.

Move your five ways while your friend watches. Then ask your friend to be your mirror. Let your mirror-friend copy you every time you move.

What did you learn about yourself? Which tells you more truth about yourself—a real mirror or a real friend?

Mimes and Truth

Mimes try to show the truth about people. They try to show the funny and sad things that people do. They try to show how people feel and think about themselves and other people.

Mimes often wear make-up and costumes. The make-up exaggerates their eyes, nose, and mouth. Why do you think mimes use make-up?

What feelings do you see in these pictures?

Can you exaggerate your walk? Try.
Can you exaggerate your smile? Try.

How does exaggeration help to show truth?

Some clowns tell jokes with words. Most clowns are mimes. They act out a joke. Which kind of clown do you enjoy more? Would you rather be a talking clown or a mime?

Clowns often wear make-up. Every clown's make-up is different.

Clowns like to make people laugh. They act and look funny. What is happening in each picture? Have you ever seen clowns do any of these things?

Often a clown does something you don't expect. A clown may make something easy to do look very hard.

Why do you laugh when you see a clown do an easy thing in a hard way? Do you sometimes do that, too? How does the clown's exaggeration help to show the truth?

When clowns fall, a stream of water may come out of their eyes. What are they exaggerating? How are they showing truth?

You, too, can exaggerate to show a truth. Show how making fun of someone may hurt.

FIRST IN
MAINTENANCE
PRODUCTS
Zep

Jesters

In Europe, long ago, there was a kind of clown called a *jester.* A jester would live in the house of a rich man.

The rich man gave the jester food and a place to live. The jester gave the rich man funny stories. He gave him funny songs and dances, too. Do you think that was fair?

The jester made people laugh. In his stories and songs, he exaggerated true feelings. His jokes and dances told people the truth about themselves.

People used to laugh at jesters. Now people laugh at clowns. Why is laughing important?

SELF EXPRESSION

Would you like to try being a clown?

First, you must decide what kind of clown you will be. Each clown has a different way of looking. Each one has a different way of walking.

You might want to put on clown make-up or wear a funny hat. Plan an act that you will do. Remember to exaggerate how you feel. Perhaps you can act out a funny story.

After you have your act ready, do it for other people. Remember not to laugh yourself! If you're laughing, people will not be able to pay attention to your act.

Ask your friends what they think of your act. Don't be hurt when people tell you what they think. You must decide what will make your act better.

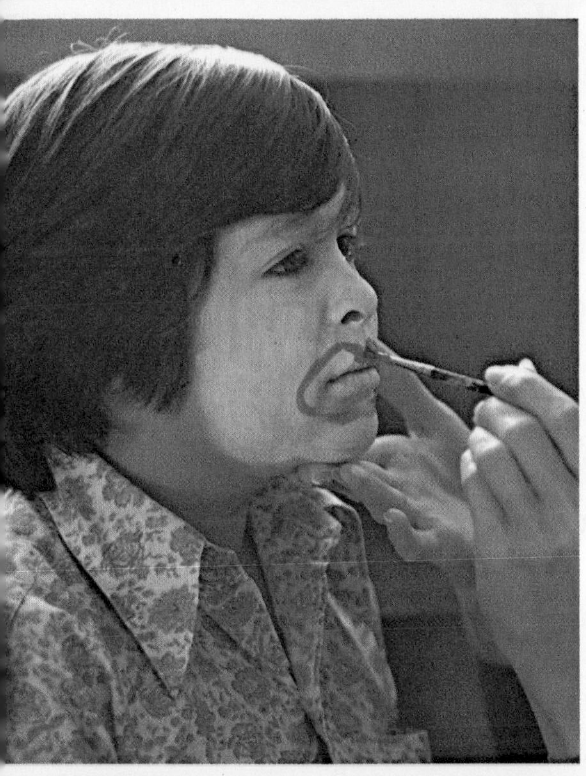
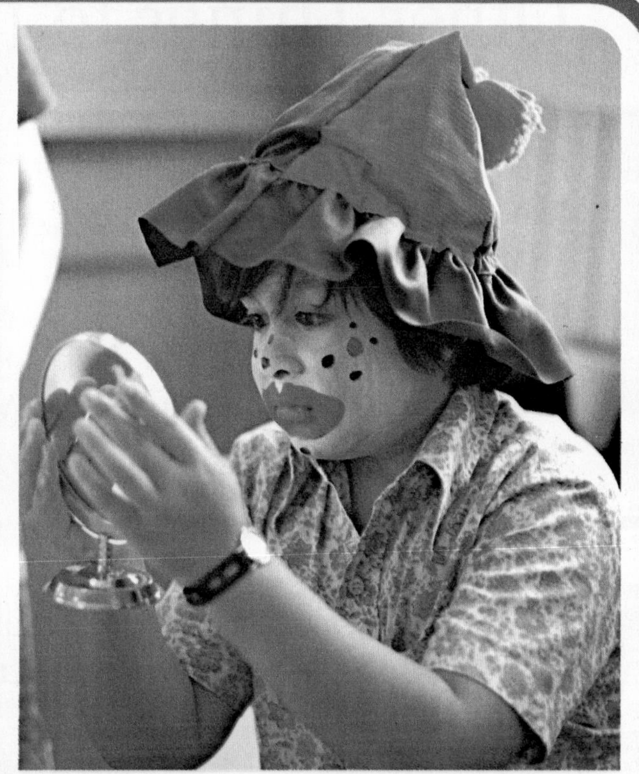

Other Things to Try

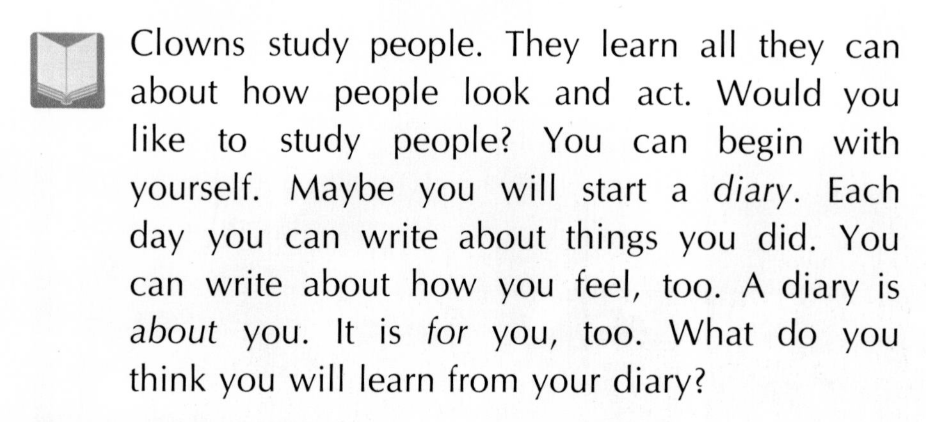

Clowns study people. They learn all they can about how people look and act. Would you like to study people? You can begin with yourself. Maybe you will start a *diary*. Each day you can write about things you did. You can write about how you feel, too. A diary is *about* you. It is *for* you, too. What do you think you will learn from your diary?

Would you like to try making up a comic strip? The people or animals in a comic strip are called *characters*. Will your characters show how people really feel and act?

Self Study

1. When do most people in your class watch television? What kinds of shows are on at that time? Do you wish there were different shows on? What can you do about it?

2. What do you think is the difference between "silly" and "funny?"

3. Sometimes it's mean to laugh. When do you think laughing is mean?

WE FIND OUT

We are in the music room at school. I heard these kids playing the guitar. I like the way a guitar sounds. Maybe Dad will teach me how to play the guitar. Then I'll be able to play both the guitar and the accordion!

My teacher is showing me how to make a pinch-pot. I am finding out a lot about clay. I think I will make this pot for my cat. She can drink water from it.

I am playing music. I am dancing at the same time. I found out this isn't too easy. I'll just keep trying until I can do it better.

One day a boy and a girl were walking along in Giantorwitchville when they saw the castle. They climbed up the hill and sneaked in the castle.

Inside the castle there were cobwebs, old curtains, dusty old chairs, couches covered with sheets and

I am typing a story I wrote. It takes me longer to type than to write. I like to learn new things. This is fun. I am going faster and faster. Oh, no! Another mistake!

I am at a 4-H meeting. I am telling people about different kinds of horses. I keep records of what Rusty does every day. I write down what he eats, too.

I am imitating my grandfather. I watch him. Then I do what he does. I may be in a show soon. I hope I'll be ready.

CARING AND TRUSTING

Babies learn and grow. You are learning and growing now. Some day you will have a job. You may get married. You will keep on learning and growing. People grow, and change, all of their lives.

Does everything change? What always stays the same? What can you count on to be always the same?

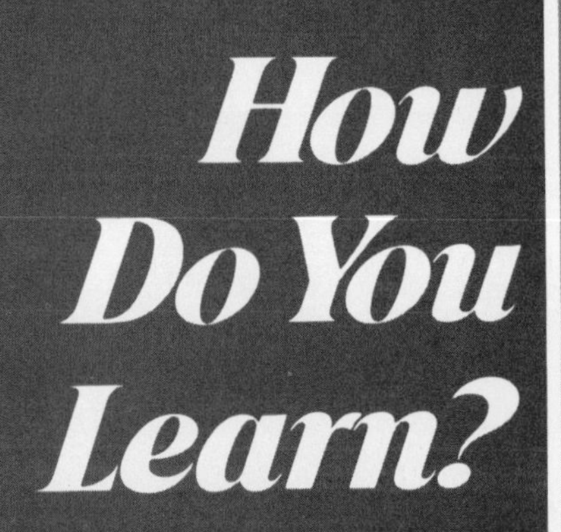

How Do You Learn?

You learn many things from other people. You teach others, too. What have you taught an animal to do? Have you ever taught someone your age? What have you taught a grown-up?

Make a list of some people in your class. Let each one write what he or she can teach. Then find something on the list that you want to learn. Take turns teaching and learning.

How do you feel when you are teaching? How do you feel when you are learning?

After you teach, think about how you did it. Did you show people how to do something your way? Did you let them find their own way? How do people like to be taught?

How would you teach a baby to say a new word? How would you teach someone to catch a ball?

There are many ways to teach. There are many ways to learn.

On Your Own

You can learn on your own.

You learn when you use your eyes. You learn when you use your ears and your nose. You learn from your sense of taste. You learn from your sense of touch.

How are these people learning?

You learn by trying something over and over. You feel so good when you can do it!

You learn from television and books. How is that different from learning on your own?

You are born knowing how to do some things. These pictures show things you don't have to learn. What other things can you think of?

Learning From People

You can learn many things on your own. You learn from other people, too. You learn by listening to others. You learn by doing what others do. You learn by *imitating* others.

Do you remember what *imitating* means? Please see page 78 if you do not.

Long ago, people did not write down their songs and stories. Instead, they passed them down from parents to children.

Parents would tell a story to their children. The children listened. They learned the story. When they grew up, they told the story to their children. How do you think they would teach songs and dances?

This story and the song that goes with it are very old. The *Winnebago* (win·uh·BAY·goh) Indians have told this story for hundreds of years. What were the Winnebago parents teaching with this story?

The *Winnebago* Indians once lived on the shores of Lake Michigan.

WAI=KUN FABLE

A *fable* is a story that teaches a lesson.

Once there were some mice under a crooked log. They believed they were the only people in the whole world. One mouse stood up and stretched his little arms. He could just touch the under side of the log. He thought that he was very tall. He thought that he had touched the sky. So he danced and sang this song.

Mo-zhu*n*-na-le,
  Pe-zhe ya-ki-ske-shun-no*n*-nink
    na-gi-kche!
Mo-zhu*n*-na-le,
  Pe-zhe ya-ki-ske shun-no*n*-nink
    na-gi-kche!
Ne-sha-na ma-*ch*i-nik-gla
  ya-ki-o-o!

Throughout the
  world
Who is there like
  little me!
Who is like me!
I can touch the sky.
I can touch the sky,
  indeed!

—Sung and told by Chash-chunk-a
(Wave, Peter Sampson)

Making Drum-Talk

American Indians often play instruments while they sing. They may drum the rhythm of a song while they sing it. When they dance, the drum helps them know how to move.

Read the song of the mouse again. Listen to the rhythm of the words. Now see if you can tap a rhythm pattern for the song. How would you make a drum say each line?

Find a rhythm that starts very tiny. Now make your rhythm grow big. How will you tap when the mouse reaches the sky?

Here are some words you can make into a drum song.

This old man,
He played one.

He played nick-nack
On my thumb.

First tap the rhythm of the words Which words will you tap loudly? You can *accent* (AK·sent) some words. That means you can give some words a heavier beat.

Write down the rhythm patterns you made up. How will you show quicker taps? How will you show heavier taps?

In your music book, a drum rhythm might look like this.

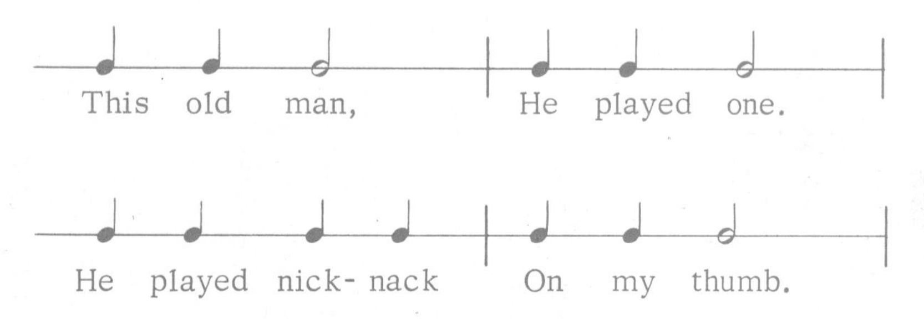

This is the way Timmy wrote his drum song. You can do it your own way.

Teach someone your song. First, play it on your drum. Then let your friends imitate your drum patterns. Now let them read and play the patterns you have written down. Which way do they like best?

SELF EXPRESSION

Perhaps you will make a book to tell about yourself. Your book might tell about some of the ways you learn.

Fold two pieces of paper. The pictures show how to do it. The outside is the cover. Put more pages inside.

On the first page, you might write some things that you like to see. Put some things that you like to hear on the second page. On other pages, you can name some things that you like to smell, taste, and touch.

Next, think about what you have learned from people. How will you show this? How will you show what you have learned in other ways?

You may want to draw pictures for your book. Work on your book until you like the way it looks. Make a book that you will want to keep for a long time.

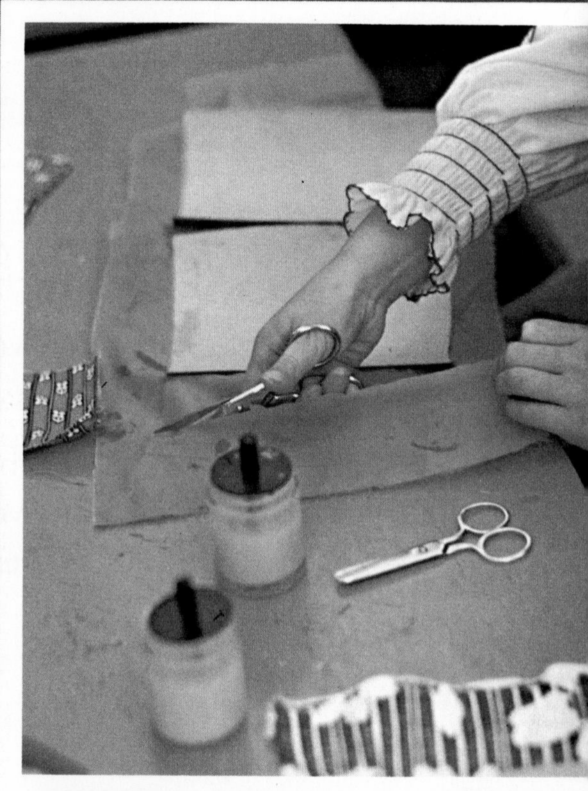

Other Things to Try

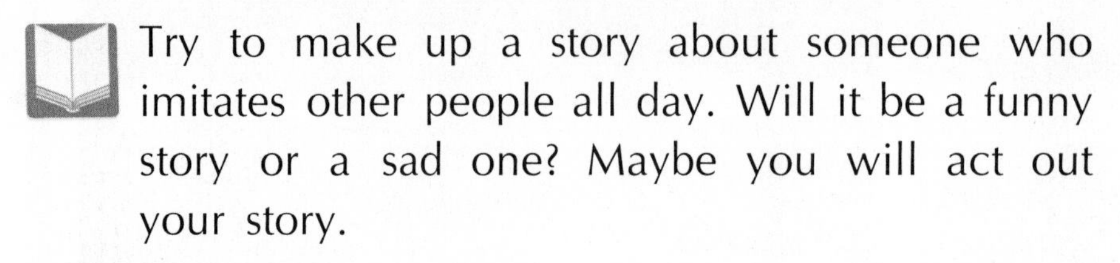

Try to make up a story about someone who imitates other people all day. Will it be a funny story or a sad one? Maybe you will act out your story.

Draw an instrument that you would like to play. Will you draw a real instrument? Will you draw something that no one has ever seen? How will you show the sounds that it makes?

Self Study

1 When is imitation a good way to learn? What could be some bad things about it? Does a kitten copy its mother? Does a mirror imitate? Can you imitate something that isn't alive? Try it. Whom do you imitate most? Who imitates you?

2 Suppose you wanted to do these things.

sing a song that you heard on the radio
make a chocolate cake
do a dance to show what you do on Saturdays
show how an elephant walks
make up a story about your friend

Would you want to imitate someone? Tell why or why not.

In these pictures, who is counting on others?
Whom do you count on?

Trusting Yourself and Others

Draw a circle on paper. Cut up the circle like pieces of a pie. Let one piece stand for what you have learned on your own. Let another piece stand for what you have learned from people your age. Make another piece for what you have learned from older people.

Make as many pieces as you need. Show all the different ways you have learned. Can you make the size of the piece show how much you have learned? Try it. Which seems to be the biggest piece?

Look at the learning pies other people have made. Are they alike in any way? How are they different?

Suppose you were twenty years old. How do you think your learning pie would be different?

When you are twenty, you may be working. You may be in school. How will you learn the job you want to have?

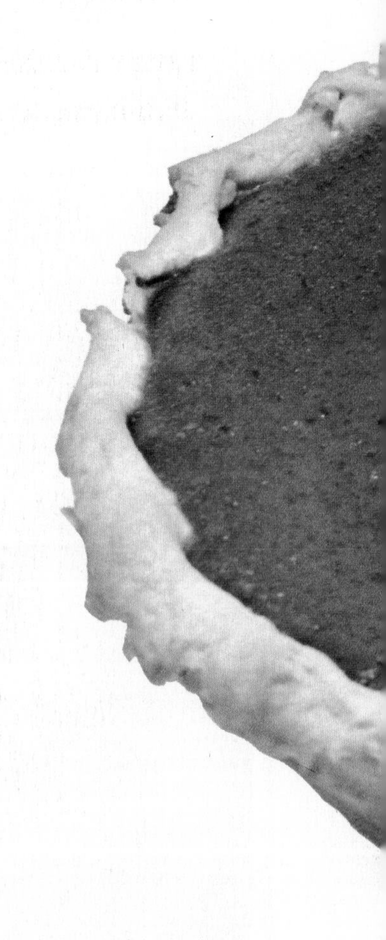

LEARNED ON
MY OWN
LEARNED FROM
OLDER PEOPLE
LEARNED FROM
PEOPLE MY AGE

Learning a Job

Suppose you were ten years old around the year 1300. Suppose you were living in a town in Europe. Suppose you wanted to be a singer when you grew up.

An *apprentice* is a learner.

First, you sign up as an *apprentice* (uh·PREN·tis) with someone who knows how to sing. You work for someone who is a master singer.

The master singer belonged to a *guild* of singers. In a guild, people all did the same kind of work. The people in the guild taught each other. They learned from one another, too. The guild made rules for how the work was to be done.

There were guilds for all kinds of work. There were guilds for hat-makers. There were guilds for people who painted pictures. There were guilds of dancers and actors.

As an apprentice you try to learn everything that the master singer can teach you. How do you think you would do this?

Craft is skill in doing a job.

You do not spend all day learning your *craft*. Sometimes you sweep the floor. You cook the food. You do whatever the master asks you to do. For a long time you receive no money. Instead you are given food and a place to live. Do you think that is fair? Why? Why not?

Making Up a Tune

Here is something you might have to do as an apprentice.

The master singer might come up to you and say, "It's time you tried to make up a song. Use two or three hand bells that play different notes. Make up a tune and sing it."

Would you like to try that? If you don't have any bells, you may use two or three keys on a piano. You may use any other melody instrument you have. You may make an instrument, too.

How will you write down your music? Write it so that someone else can play it. This is the way some people your age wrote their songs. You may write your music in notes like the ones in your music book. If you want to, you may do it your own way.

How will you show which notes should be played? How will you show when the music goes up? How will you show when the music goes down? Will your notes always take one step at a time? Will they sometimes jump a step?

Now play and sing your song for someone. Do you think the apprentice always pleased the master? Whom do you like to please? When is it just as important to please yourself?

The Next Step

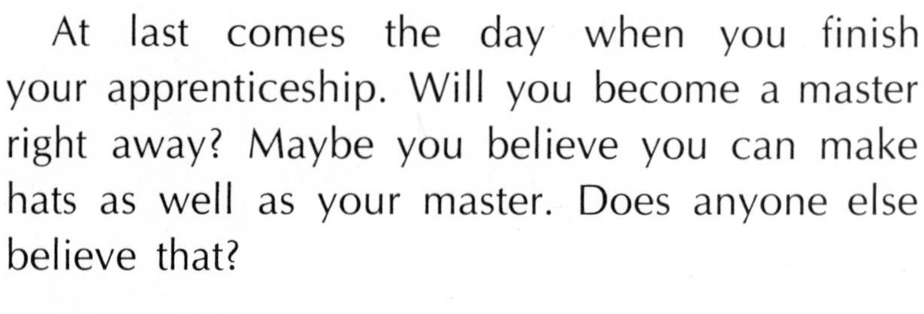

At last comes the day when you finish your apprenticeship. Will you become a master right away? Maybe you believe you can make hats as well as your master. Does anyone else believe that?

All of the guilds had different rules. In most guilds you would next become a *journeyman.* As a journeyman, you work by the day. You keep on learning.

Sometimes it is hard to get a job where people do not know you. If they know your work, they believe you can do the job. They trust you. They have *faith* in you.

At last, you think you are ready to become a master. You have faith in yourself. You hope that many people have faith in you.

You carefully prepare a *masterpiece,* the best work that you can do. If you make tables, you make a table as well as you can. If you are a dancer, you make up a beautiful dance. Then, you ask some masters in the guild to see your masterpiece. If they think it is good enough, you, too, can become a master.

How do you think you would have liked being in a guild? Do you think guilds were fair? Where can you find more about guilds?

How do people learn their jobs today? The woman in the top picture is learning to be a carpenter. Can you tell what the man in the bottom picture is learning? Whom do they have faith in?

SELF EXPRESSION

IN THE MIDEAST

A class of children in York, Pennsylvania, set up a guild in their classroom. Your class might want to divide into three or four guilds.

How will you decide what your guild will make or do? Will you make belts or pictures? Will you make up dances?

Next, you must find someone who will teach you the craft you need. Where will you find your master craftsman? Perhaps a mother or father of someone in the class can help.

Perhaps you know an older child who can teach the skill you need. What kind of master will you choose? What kinds of people can you learn from?

In the old days, the guilds sometimes sold what they made at fairs. The guilds of artists, dancers, and musicians gave shows at fairs, too. You might want to have a fair some time.

SKIN
Pottery Guild
AND
BONES

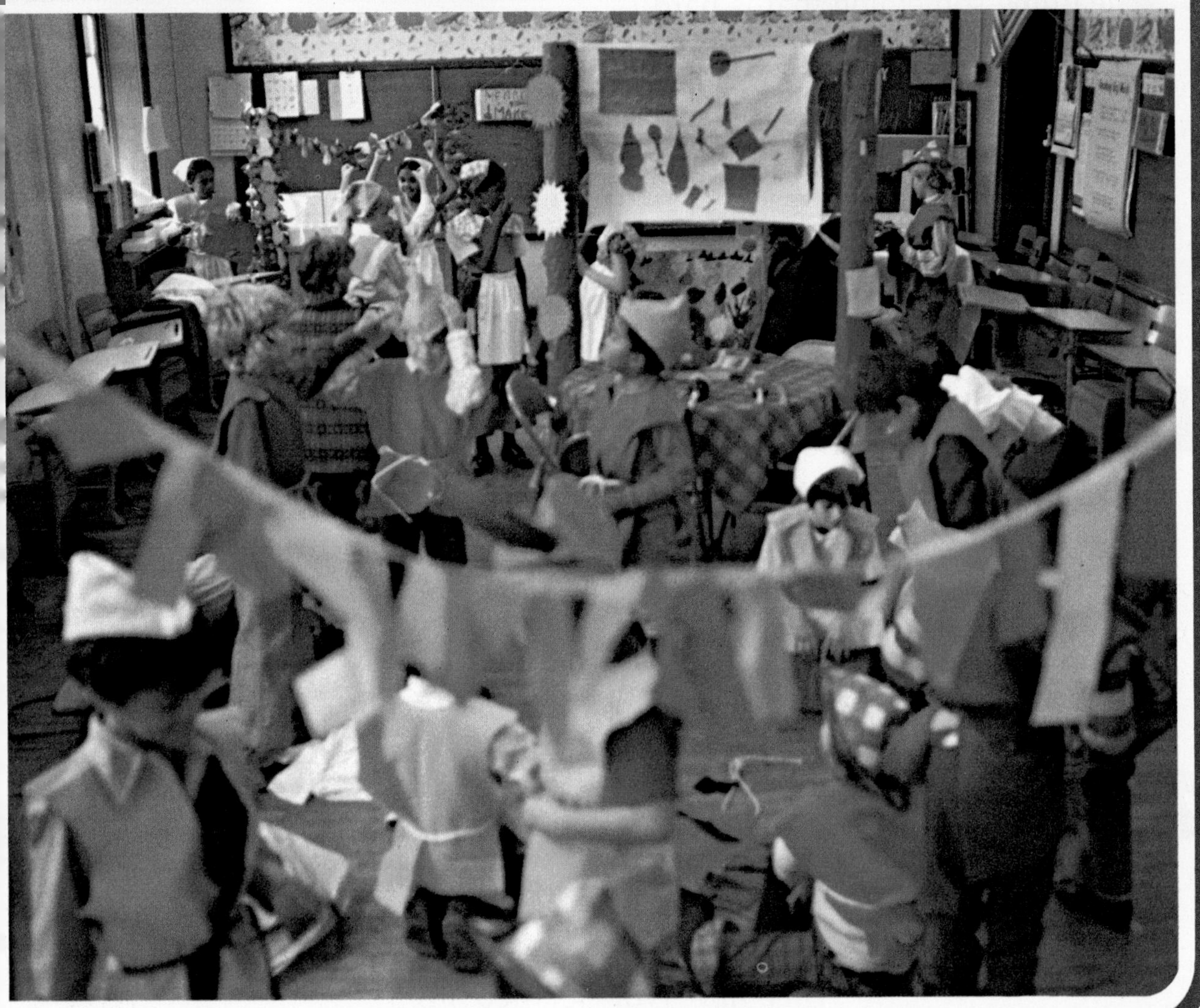

Other Things to Try

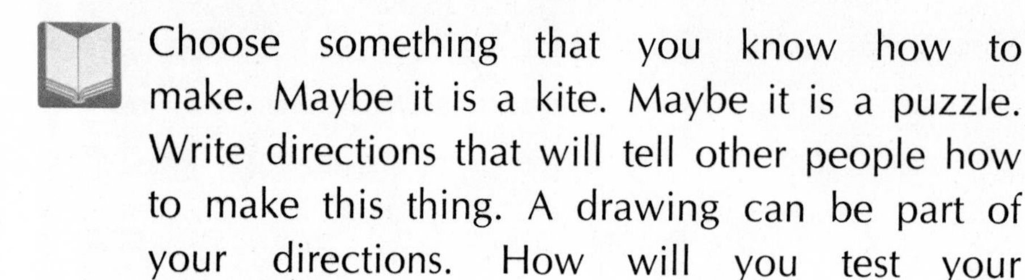

Choose something that you know how to make. Maybe it is a kite. Maybe it is a puzzle. Write directions that will tell other people how to make this thing. A drawing can be part of your directions. How will you test your directions?

Draw a picture of yourself learning something that is fun. Draw another picture of yourself learning something that is hard.

Self Study

1 Suppose you tried to carve a dog's head out of soap. Would you be able to do it well the first time? As you try to do things well, you may make many mistakes. Each mistake tells you about something that will not work. Each mistake tells you to try still another way. How do mistakes make you feel? Have you ever made a funny mistake?

2 If you could learn anything in the world, what would you learn? Whom would you choose to be your teacher?

What have you learned from the people you love?

Learning Together

Belinda and Roland Villanueva live in San Antonio, Texas. At school they learn many of the same things you learn. School is not the only place where Belinda and Roland learn. Like you, they learn at home, too.

Belinda and Roland learned to speak Spanish at home. Their grandmother taught them. She is teaching them how to make *tortillas* (tohr·TEE·ahs), also. What is their father teaching in the middle picture?

Tortillas are flat cakes made of cornmeal.

Belinda and Roland teach, too. They are teaching their little cousin, Manuel, to speak English. He just came from Mexico this year. They teach the younger children in their family many things, also.

People in a family teach and learn from one another all the time. Mothers and fathers teach their children by what they say. They teach them by how they act, too.

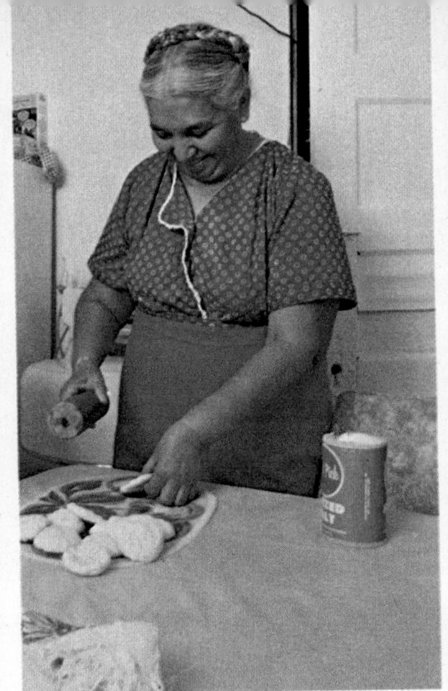

Belinda and Roland will always remember the stories and sayings they hear at home. Here are some Mexican American sayings:

> *A dios rogando y con el mazo dando.*
> Pray to God but keep working hard.
>
> *La mansa respuesta quebranta la ira.*
> A soft reply breaks up anger.

Can you guess why Belinda and Roland like to speak Spanish? Say the Spanish word *respuesta* (res·PWAYS·tuh). Then say the English word "reply." You can hear how different it feels to speak Spanish.

Mr. and Mrs. Villanueva teach their children what they believe. What do they teach through these sayings?

Try to think of sayings that you hear at home. Write them down. Perhaps you would like to tell about some things your family thinks are important.

From Many Lands

All over the world, children are taught what their families know and believe in. You learn some things at home. You learn some in school. Where else do you learn them?

There are so many different kinds of people in the United States. People come here from many other lands. All of these people bring different ideas with them. They bring different foods. They bring different languages, different songs and dances, too. Together, people learn from one another.

Proverbs (PROV·urbs) say things that people believe. The Mexican American sayings on page 195 are proverbs. People all over the world have proverbs.

There are thousands of proverbs. You may have heard these sayings.

The early bird catches the worm.

When the cat's away, the mice will play.

A proverb means more than it seems to mean. Can you tell what these proverbs mean?

In Africa there are many groups of people. Each group has proverbs of its own. Sometimes proverbs are used to praise people. Often they are used to warn people. Sometimes they are used to make fun of people. In some African groups, children are not allowed to say proverbs to grown-ups.

African groups are very different from one another. However, their proverbs are very much alike. Why do you think that is so? Here are some African proverbs.

Yoruba

Ewe

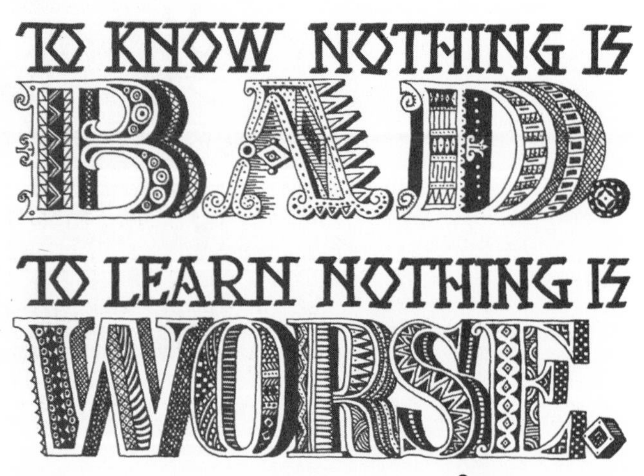

Serer

Does your family believe these things, too?

You can make up a saying about a belief that people share. Only your great, great grandchildren will know if you made up a proverb. Suppose, in the year 2500, thousands of families were repeating your saying. That means you would have made up a proverb.

A proverb must tell something that people in a group believe. It must be easy to remember. If it has an interesting sound, people will enjoy repeating it. Many proverbs have words that rhyme. "Haste makes waste." Some proverbs have a rhythm that is easy to remember. "Never trouble trouble 'til trouble troubles you." Some proverbs have words in them that sound alike. "Birds of a feather flock together."

Which words in these proverbs rhyme? Which words start with the same letter?

When you make up a proverb, you make music with words. A proverb has rhythm. It has interesting sounds.

Try to play some proverbs on a music instrument. What instruments do certain words make you think of? Can you clap the rhythm of all the words together? How does making music help you to remember proverbs?

Sayings Today

People in the United States have sayings and proverbs, too. Today the sayings people seem to know best are *slogans*. Slogans on T-shirts, posters, and buttons may tell what people believe in.

A slogan is a saying that many people like. Because they like it, they say it. A slogan often does not tell what a group believes. A slogan may not last very long either. How are the slogans on page 201 different from proverbs?

People tell about their beliefs in proverbs. They also tell what they believe and feel in their music and dance. Almost everything people do shows something about how they think and feel.

The people that you know help you grow. You help the people you know to grow. What do you think all of you will be like ten years from now? What will always be the same? What will change?

Try to find some of the art that you did when you were very young. What do you see that tells you that it was you who did this art? Ask other children to show what they did as young children. Can you tell which art was done by certain children? How does your art look different from the art the others did? What things are the same about everybody's paintings?

Milk has something for every body.

HAVE YOU THANKED A GREEN PLANT TODAY?

Only You Can Prevent Forest Fires

SELF EXPRESSION

You and your friends can make a big picture together. Perhaps you will make a *mural* (MYOOR·uhl). A mural is a painting done on a wall. Perhaps you can paint on a piece of large brown paper. Then you can hang the paper on a wall.

Instead of a mural, you might want to make a *mosaic*. A mosaic is made of bits of colored stones or glass. Can you tell which picture on page 203 is a mosaic?

You might want to paint a picture of things you have learned. Your painting might show how you learned them. Perhaps you will make a picture that shows what you and your family think is important. You might want to paint what people in your country believe, too.

What idea will you and your friends choose? How will you decide who will work where?

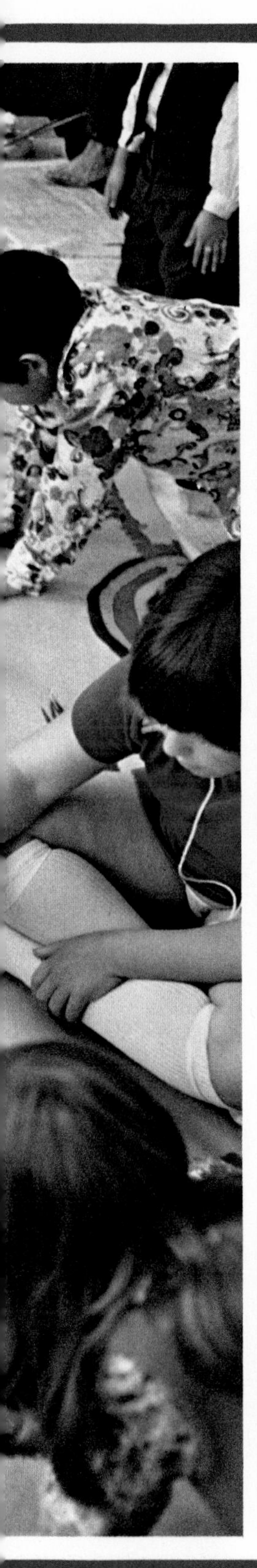

ANIMALS
ZOO

SCHOOL BUS
STOP
1970
ALVARADO

Other Things to Try

A group can make up a funny play that ends with a proverb. Think of a time when a family might say "An apple a day keeps the doctor away." You might want to use a different proverb. Act out your play in front of the class. Perhaps you will let the class guess what the proverb is.

What if you could hear people speaking all over the world? This would be a really great chorus of sounds. Take just one word like "yes." Find out how other languages say "yes." You could make a world chorus by fitting many kinds of "yes" words together. What different rhythms will you hear? Take turns making up music for your world chorus. How will you end the music?

Self Study

1 Why do you think people wear names and slogans on T-shirts and buttons? What slogans do you like to wear?

2 If you moved to another place, would you still believe the same things you believe now? What would be different?

What do you wonder about?

A Great Wonder

People wonder about stars.

They wonder about wild things in the forest.

They wonder about plants and animals in the sea.

They wonder about life in growing things.

The human body is a wonder.
Love is a wonder.
Indeed, this world is a place of wonder.
What do you wonder about?

Wonders of Space

Do you ever wonder about yourself?

Who are you? Write three sentences that tell who you are. Start each sentence with the words "I am." After you have written your sentences, share them with others. How do people see themselves?

Here is another way of looking at yourself. You are one of more than three and a half billion people living on the Earth. Earth is one of nine planets moving around the sun. The Sun is a star, one of trillions of stars.

Have you ever tried to count the stars you can see? Counting stars can make you dizzy!

Long ago, people thought they saw shapes in the stars. They wondered about the shapes. They made up stories about them. Today people call these shapes *constellations* (kon·stuh·LAY·shuns). How many constellations have you seen?

On a clear night, some stars seem very close. They are really far, far away. Suppose a space ship could travel at the speed of light. It would still take four years to get to the star closest to the sun.

All the stars you can see are in the same *galaxy* (GAL·uk·see). A galaxy is a very large group of stars. You can see just one part of your galaxy. The part you see is called the Milky Way. There are millions and millions of stars just in the Milky Way. There are more than 10 billion galaxies in outer space!

Do you feel like getting back to Earth? Just turn the page!

Wonders of Earth

Earth is a place of wonders, too.

There are more than one million different kinds of animals on Earth. There are more than 300,000 different kinds of plants. Every year new kinds of plants and animals are discovered. Every year some plants and animals become *extinct*.

When something becomes *extinct* it dies out and never is seen alive again.

These are places of wonder in the United States. Which ones have you seen? Perhaps you will tell the class about a wonderful place you have been. Perhaps you will tell about a wonderful animal you have seen.

There is so much to wonder about in the world. Wonders make some people feel small. Wonders can make people feel important, too.

Long ago in Hawaii, when a royal child was born, people chanted a religious poem. Dancing was an important part of the old Hawaiian religion. The pictures show how this poem might have been danced.

The poem named all the animals and plants that the Hawaiians knew. It told how the gods made all things for men and women to use. It told how the child was related to all the wonders of the world. This is part of the poem.

In time, men multiplied,
In time, men came from afar.
Born were the fair-haired,
Born the dark-haired,
Born were the broad-chested,
Born the big eaters.
Born were the song-chanters,
Born the family men.
Born were war leaders,
Born the high chiefs of long life.
Ever increasing in number,
  men spread abroad.
Man was here now; it was DAY.

What did the Hawaiians think was the greatest wonder of all?

You are not a royal child. Still, you, and other children, too, are the most important wonder of all.

In the year 2000, you will be men and women. The world will then be yours. How will you take care of the world? How will you keep it safe? How will you protect plants and animals? Perhaps you will find out more about outer space. Then you will have even more to care for.

This will be a big job. But people all over the Earth have faith in children.

Mothers and fathers teach their children to have faith in themselves. They teach them to have faith in good people. They teach them to have faith in the beliefs that they live by.

Dancing began as an act of faith. Like the Hawaiians long ago, many people have danced when they worshipped their gods.

Some dances today still show what people believe in. José Limon (hoh·ZAY lee·MOHN) made up a beautiful dance called *There is a Time*.

The dance is done to these words from *Ecclesiastes* (ee·clee·zee·AS·tees).

Ecclesiastes is a book in the Bible.

To every thing there is a season, and a time to every purpose under the heaven:
A time to be born, and a time to die; a time to plant, and a time to pluck up that which is planted;
A time to kill, and a time to heal; a time to break down, and a time to build up;
A time to weep and a time to laugh; a time to mourn, and a time to dance. . . .

This is your time to learn. There is plenty of time.

SELF EXPRESSION

What do you wonder about? You might want to make up a dance to tell what you wonder. First, think about what you wonder. Then decide how you will move to dance that wondering.

Your wondering might be about something very big. It might be, "I wonder what makes the sky blue." Your wondering might be about something very small. It could be, "I wonder what I'll have for dinner tonight."

The child in the top row of pictures wondered, "What makes thunder?" The child in the bottom row is answering, "Giants rolling a bowling ball."

Perhaps another person will dance an answer to your wondering. It may be a funny answer. It may be a true answer.

Your wonder question will be only part of your dance. How will you begin your dance? How will you end it?

Other Things to Try

Take some clay. With it in your hands, think about what you wonder. Make something that will remind you of what you wonder.

Why does a peach have fuzz on it? How did love come into the world? Why are dogs such good friends to people? Try to make up answers for these questions. Perhaps you will write your answer as part of a story.

Self Study

1 How do you think people from another galaxy might look? How do you think they might act? Would you rather have them *look* like Earth people or *act* like Earth people? Which do you think is more important?

2 The Hawaiians said, "In time, men multiplied." What about women? Why do you think the Hawaiians did not say, "In time, men and women multiplied"?

WE LEARN

I am learning to make my own pictures. Here I am in the darkroom. It is at our school. My teacher showed me how to do this. I love to see the pictures appear. It's like magic!

I am teaching a folk dance I learned. I read about it in a book. The book told about dances from around the world. I like to learn about other countries.

My mom made this clown outfit for me. I am going to be in the show today. I am scared! Dad is saying, "Don't worry. You've done this act over and over. I know you'll be good."

My teacher is showing me how to play. He is a friend of my father. He plays a song. Then he shows me how to play it. I am learning a Texas song. We live in Texas.

I am making an animal out of clay. I learned how to do this by myself. Animals are easier to do than pots. I'll get back to pots in a minute.

Dad and Mom are watching me ride. Dad wants to be sure I can handle Rusty. Dad and Mom are both very good riders. The Fair is next week. I can hardly wait.

CARING ABOUT FAIRNESS

Fair can mean beautiful.

Fair can mean pretty good.

Fair can mean a place where things are sold. People have a good time at fairs.

Fair can mean right and honest.

What does *fair* mean to you?

Same or Different?

These people all belong to the same family. How are they all alike? How are they different?

All of these children are seven, eight, or nine years old. How are they all alike? How are they different?

Everyone is just like everyone else in some important ways. How are these children alike? Everyone is different in important ways, too. How are these children different?

When you were born, you were already different from all other babies. As you grow up, you become more different from other people. That's because each person has a different kind of life. The things that happen to you help to make you *you*.

Think of something important that has happened to you. Think of something that has made you *you*. How will you share this with others? Perhaps you will paint a picture. Perhaps you will act out an event in your life. Find a way to tell what makes you different.

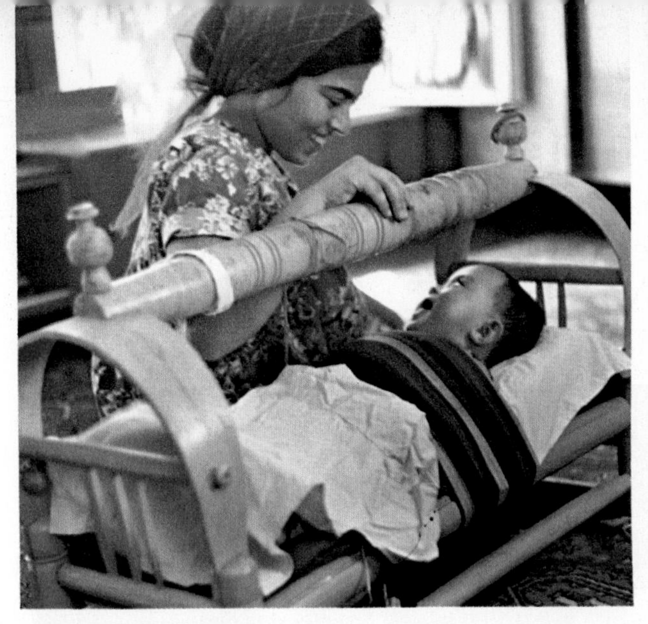

Signs of Feelings

Can you tell how the people in these pictures feel? What are the signs?

Everyone has feelings.

People in the same family sometimes show their feelings in the same way. People who live in the same place also may show their feelings in the same way. They may speak and move in the same way. Why do you think this is so?

Eskimo Styles

This Arctic Eskimo hunts sea animals through ice holes. When he dances, he stands in one place. He moves up and down. He dances in the same way he hunts.

Hunting is very important to the Arctic Eskimos. They praise hunters in all the things they make. Many of their stories tell about great hunters. Carvings like these tell about the deeds of hunters, too.

Here is an Eskimo song. This is how the Eskimos would write it down.

Qimmiapik's Song ᑭᒥᐊᐱᒃ ᐱᓯᒐ

ᓇᓄᐊᓕᓗᒐᔪᒐ ᑐᒋᓚᐊ

ᓇᓄᐊᓕᓗᒐᔪᒐ ᑐᒋᓚᐅᐸᒐ ᐁ ᔭ ᔭ ᔭ ᔭᐊ

ᓄᐃᓗᑲ ᓄᑭᑲᒋᒪᓂ ᐊᓄᓇᔪᒐ ᐅᒪᓕᑐᒥ

ᓄᐃᓗᑲ ᓄᑭᑲᒋᒪᓂ

ᓇᓄᐊᓕᓗᒐᔪᒐ ᑐᒋᓚᐅᐸᒐ ᐁ ᔭ ᔭ ᔭ ᔭᐊ

nanualirlungayunga tungilaa	I saw a polar bear. I did. Way down there,
nanualirlungayunga tungilaukpaunga	I saw a polar bear. I did.
ai yai yai yai yaa	I was way down there.
niulukka nukigangimani	My weak legs not having any strength,
anunayunga umalirktumi	I put on the dogs' harness with pounding heart,
niulukka nukigangimani	My weak legs not having any strength,
nanualirlungayunga tungilaukpaunga	I saw a polar bear. I did.
ai yai yai yai yaa	I was way down there.

——Recorded and translated by Nelson Graburn

we saw seven whales and Most of them were pilot whales but that was still all right. Just if we see whales it was all right, all right, all right, all right! Just if we see whales!

I saw a whale and it was Big. it was a very, very Big Whale. so I saw a gray whale and It was a Baby whale too!

Rosa

I wish I saw a whale That was a dragon. I wish, I wish, I do wish, yes, I do wish!

Each group has its own *style*. When you paint or dance you use the style of your group. You are different from all other people, too. You have a style all your own.

Style is the way something is done. A group's style comes from the things the group thinks are important.

Children your age wrote these songs about whales. Their teacher wrote down the notes. See how different the songs are. Can you sing and play each song?

SELF EXPRESSION

Make up a dance that shows different ways you can move. First, think about how you will use your hands and arms. Show some big ways you move your hands and arms every day. Now show some little ways you move.

Now how do you want to move your head? See how many different ways you can move it. Choose one way to show some other children.

See how many different ways you can stretch your whole body. Find some ways to move while sitting down. Find some different ways to move while jumping.

Watch how each person moves. Does everyone choose a different way to move?

Why is there so much difference? Perhaps your dance will show how you feel, too. Show how you feel about being like other people. Show how you feel about being different.

Other Things to Try

Find a painting in this book. Find out how five people feel about the painting. Make a list of the words that the people use to tell how they feel. Do they all feel the same way about the painting? What feelings do the five people share about the painting?

Some people talk to each other in sign language. See if you can talk to someone just by using signs. You can make up your own signs to do this. How will the other person know what your signs mean?

Self Study

1. Is it good to know about other people's styles? Should you just study about your own country? Why or why not?

2. Some people like to wear clothes that look like the clothes their friends wear. Others try to dress differently. What kinds of clothes do you like to wear? When do you like to look like everyone else? When do you like to look different? How different do you like to look?

What rules are people following in each picture?

Freedom and Order

These children are playing an old Mexican game. It is called *colorinas* (co·lo·REE·naz). *Colorinas* is played with beans. First the children try to throw beans into a hole.

This player takes the beans. She throws them into the air. She catches some on the back of her hand. She throws them again. She catches them in her hand. The person who has the most beans at the end is the winner.

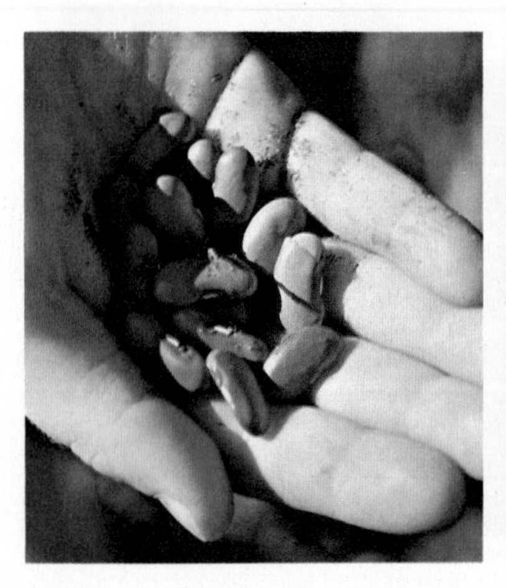

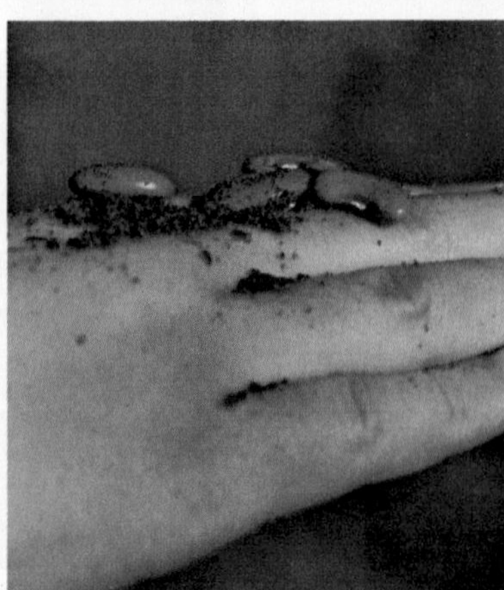

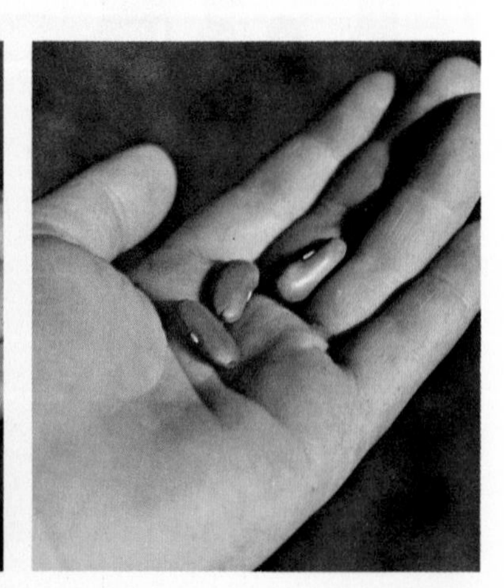

How is *colorinas* like marbles or jacks? How is it different? You may know many ways to play jacks and marbles. The rules for each game are different.

Can you make up a new game? Write down the rules.

Now teach your game to someone. Be sure to explain your rules. Suppose your friend doesn't like your rules. What will you do?

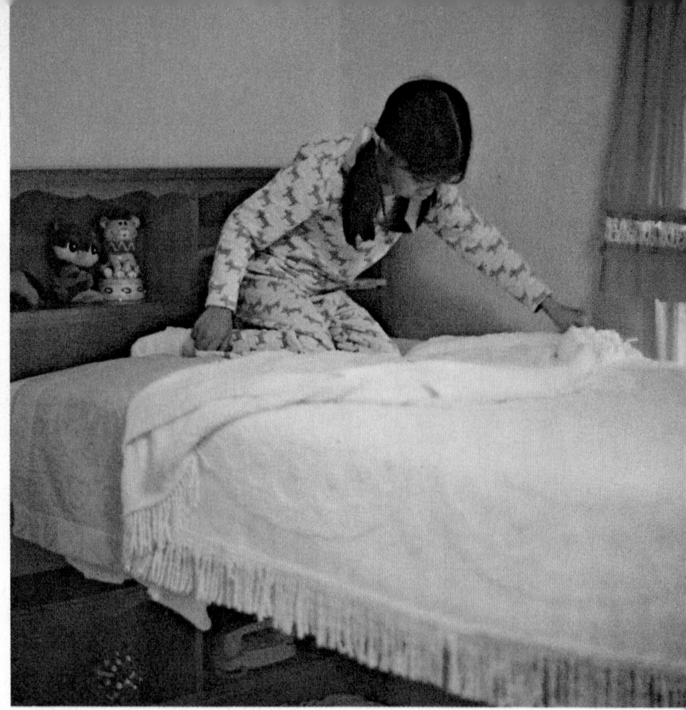

These pictures tell about rules. What rules do they tell about? Who made each rule?

Games have rules. Families have rules. Countries have rules. Some rules are written down on paper. Other rules are written only in people's hearts. They are understood even though they are not written down on paper. Sometimes unwritten rules are just as important as written rules.

Rules are different in different countries. These pictures were taken in *Liberia*. They tell about a rule that is important to the Kpelle people. Among the Kpelle, children must help grown-ups. That is an unwritten rule that the Kpelle children obey.

Liberia is a country in Africa. Did you remember that?

Here are some other rules that are important to Kpelle children.

Speak to grown-ups only when they speak to you first.

Obey all the older people in your family.

Why do you think these rules were made? Do these rules seem fair to you? It is hard to know if other people's rules are fair. Why do you think that is so?

Rules in Poetry

There are rules for writing some poems, too. There are many different ways to make up poems. People who write poems decide what rules they will use for each poem they write. Writers use rules that will help them say what they want to say.

Some writers use a rhyming rule. *Rhymes* are words that end with the same sounds, like *tree* and *knee*. Some writers use a rhythm rule. Can you clap the rhythm of this poem?

From "Every Time I Climb a Tree"

Every time I climb a tree
I scrape a leg
Or skin a knee.

—David McCord

The rhyme rule for this poem is: rhyme the first and third lines. What is the rhythm rule for this poem?

The writer decides what his or her rules will be. Each writer's rules may be different from those of any other writer. Writers often break their rules, too. After all, what a poem says is most important.

Here is a different kind of poem.

Galloping pony—
alone, against the moonlight,
on a whitened beach.

—Kyorai

Waterfall, only
a foot high, makes a large cool
music at evening.

—Issa

These poems come from Japan. They were written a long time ago. These poems are called *haiku* (hiy·KOO).

What are some rules for writing haiku? See if you can figure them out. Then turn the page to see what they are.

These are the rules for writing haiku in Japanese.

There are seventeen *syllables* in the whole poem. Syllables are the parts of a word. When you say a word, you can hear the parts it is divided into, like *gal-lop-ing*. How many syllables does the word *galloping* have?

The first line of a haiku has five syllables.

Galloping pony—
Uma-no-ko no

The second line has seven syllables.

alone, against the moonlight,
hama kake-mawaru

The third line has five syllables.

on a whitened beach.
tsuki-yo kana

A haiku has just three lines. At the right you can see the way the "Galloping pony" haiku looks in Japanese writing. Japanese writing is read from up to down and from right to left.

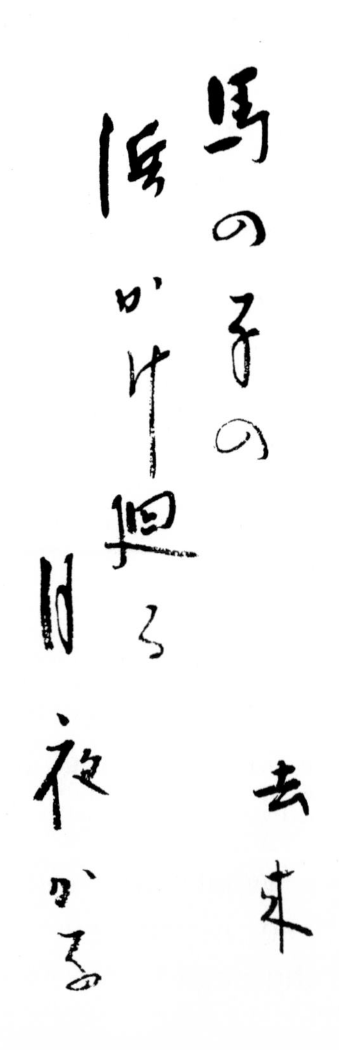

Each haiku tells you just a little about something. The painting on this page is Japanese, too. How is the painting like haiku?

There are many other kinds of poetry. There are many ways to paint and dance, too. People all over the world have different ways and different rules for doing things. You will find out about these as you grow up.

There is no one *right* way to paint or to dance or to make music. As you grow older you will find some ways that seem right for you. Perhaps you will make up some new ways.

There is one unwritten rule followed by all artists. They try not to copy each other's work. If they ever do, they tell who first did the work. Why is this fair?

SELF EXPRESSION

The pictures show haiku that were written by people your age. Like many Japanese haiku, these poems were written about the seasons.

Some children in Connecticut wrote haiku, too. They wrote their haiku together as a class. Here is a haiku they wrote.

Love all your neighbors.
A warm and tender feeling—
Love is really good.

You can write a haiku about a season or about a feeling. The writer of haiku often tries to show something in nature to the reader.

You can write haiku alone or with other people. Will you keep the haiku rules? If you don't, will your poem still be haiku?

Perhaps you will make up a new kind of poem.

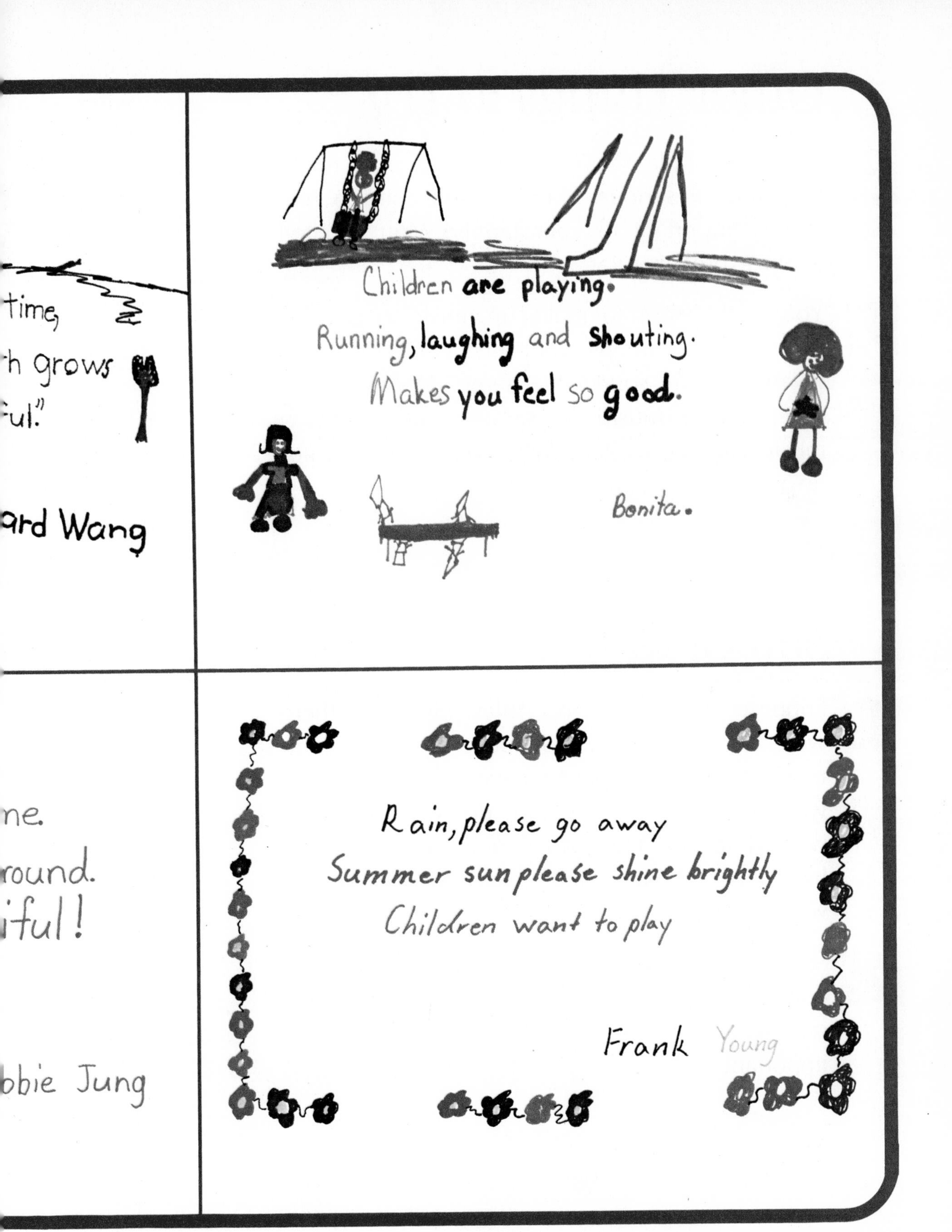

Children are playing.
Running, laughing and shouting.
Makes you feel so good.
Bonita.
Rain, please go away
Summer sun please shine brightly
Children want to play
Frank Young

Other Things to Try

Make up a play about rules. Your play might be funny or serious. Will you tell about a rule that is important to your family? Will you tell about a broken rule?

You might want to make up music to go with your haiku. Perhaps your first and third lines of music will sound the same. Making every other line of music the same is just one way music can be written. What other music rules do you know about?

Self Study

1 Suppose there were no rules. Suppose there were no written laws. Suppose there were no unwritten laws either. You would be free then, wouldn't you? You could do whatever you wanted to do. How do you think you would like that? What would happen if everyone were free?

2 Some rules are very important. Other rules don't matter as much. What rules are most important to you? What rules are not so important?

What is important to each child in these pictures? How do you know?

Your Own Code

Do you know who any of these men and women are? What do you know about them? Each of these people has done something for others. Each one is a *hero*. A *hero* is someone that many people admire.

Whom do you look up to? Is there someone you want to be like? Why do you admire that person?

Heroes act in ways that show what they believe in. Heroes make rules for themselves. Then they try to live by those rules.

Some heroes are given honors. Often, parades are held for them. Everyone knows who some heroes are. Other heroes may be known to just a few people.

Now look at these pictures at the left. Can you tell what each person thinks is important? Could these people be called heroes too? Is someone born a hero?

Heroes sometimes have a *motto* (MOT·oh) that they follow. A motto tells what a person or a group believes in. Sometimes a motto is a word, like *Fairness*. Sometimes it is a sentence. *Be Prepared* is the motto of the Boy Scouts.

Think of a rule that your hero lives by. Can you make up a motto for your hero?

Japanese Heroes

The puppets in this picture are called *Bunraku* (bun·RA·koo) puppets. *Bunraku* puppets are three to four feet tall. It takes three people to move each puppet.

This puppet play is about some Japanese heroes. These Japanese heroes are called *samurai* (SAM·uh·riy). Suppose you had lived in Japan in the year 1200. You would probably have admired the samurai. The samurai were a group of soldiers. They were called "masters of the art of war."

Why do you think some people admire soldiers? Do you know someone who has fought in a war? What kind of person makes a good soldier?

Each samurai was faithful to his own leader. He fought the samurai of other leaders.

The samurai made up rules for themselves. A set of rules is called a *code*. The samurai code was called *bushido* (bush·EE·doh).

Bushido was more important to the samurai than anything else. The *bushido* code said that a samurai must be very brave. He must be ready to meet death at any time.

Each samurai had to be a good example for the people. The code said that each samurai should try to be a master of the art of peace, too. The samurai promised to study art and history. They promised to be kind to the poor and weak. They promised to live simply and to be honest.

Knights and Chivalry

In the year 1200 in Europe, there were many fighting men called *knights* (NITES).

Suppose that you had lived in Europe in the year 1200. Would you have admired the knights? Would you have wanted to be a knight yourself some day? Before you decide, you'll want to know what knights believed in. You'll want to know what rules they lived by.

A knight had to be the son of another knight. At age seven, a young boy was sent to another man's castle. He became a *page*. A page learned to use a sword. He learned how to ride a horse.

At age fourteen, a page became a *squire* (SKWIRE). A squire helped his master put on armor. This was a big job. Armor weighed up to one hundred pounds. The squire kept the armor polished and repaired. He rode to battle with the knight. He carried the knight's sword.

A squire was taught the rules of *chivalry* (SHIV·uhl·ree). Chivalry was the code the knight obeyed. A knight must be polite. He must be brave and faithful. He must be fair. He must be kind to the weak.

Not every squire could become a knight. First, the squire had to show his bravery in battle. For twenty-four hours before the ceremony that would make him a knight, the squire did not eat. He prayed. He thought about what it would mean to be a knight. Then the ceremony took place. His master would tap the young squire with a sword. His master would say, "Be a good knight."

How was chivalry like *bushido?* Which rules do you admire? Which rules of the knights would you choose for yourself?

Girls were not allowed to be knights or samurai. Neither were the children of poor people. Do you think that was fair?

Have you ever seen a *coat of arms* before? Knights used to wear a coat of arms to show who they were.

Do you remember what *symbols* are? See page 96 if you don't.

The symbols and colors in the coat of arms stood for things that the knight believed in. Sometimes they stood for things that happened to him. The symbols could be of people, animals, or things.

Values are ideas that people think are most important.

People also made up symbols for *values* that they believed in. Values like truth, beauty, love, faith, and justice have always been important to many people. Knights may have used symbols for these values on their *shields*. A star might stand for truth. You know that a heart can stand for love. What other symbols can you make up for truth, beauty, love, faith, and justice?

A *shield* was a part of a knight's armor. The knight carried the shield for protection.

You can make up a coat of arms for yourself. You can make up your own symbols for it. What is important to you? What symbols will you choose for your coat of arms?

First, draw a shield. If you want to, divide the shield into four parts. You can put a different symbol in each part.

Now think about how you will tell about yourself. Here are some ideas.

You can draw a symbol for something you are good at.

You can draw a symbol for something you want to be good at.

You can draw a symbol for something you believe is important.

Under the symbols you might want to write your motto.

SELF EXPRESSION

IN THE WEST

Some children in Wilson, Wyoming, had read about King Arthur and the Knights of the Round Table.

They had read about the code of chivalry. They knew that each knight tried to do kind acts for people. Each one wanted to prove that he was a true and good knight. King Arthur thought that knights should prove this by good deeds, not by fighting.

The children in Wilson decided to set up a Round Table. They decided to help some old people who lived near their school. The pictures show some of the things they did.

You and your friends can set up a Round Table, too. First, decide what code you want to follow. Suppose you don't agree on the code? What is a fair way to decide?

Think of something that will do good for others. Perhaps your Round Table will help younger children. Perhaps it will make your school a better place.

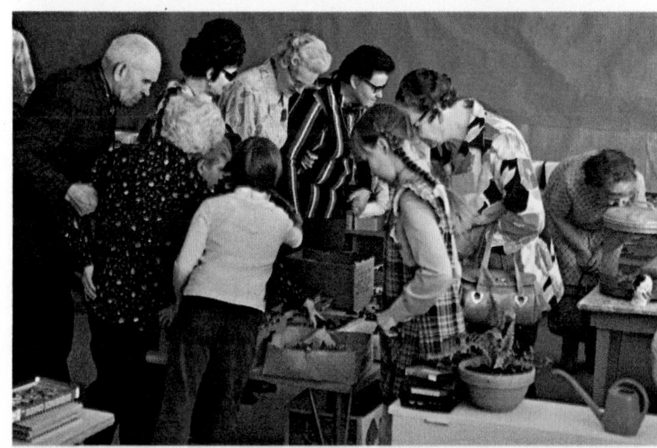

Other Things to Try

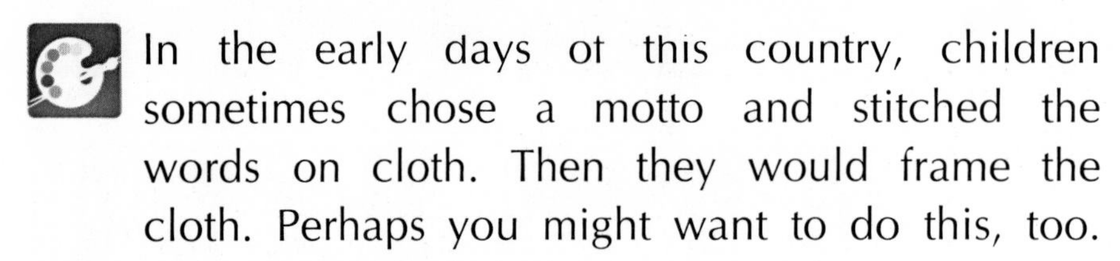

In the early days of this country, children sometimes chose a motto and stitched the words on cloth. Then they would frame the cloth. Perhaps you might want to do this, too.

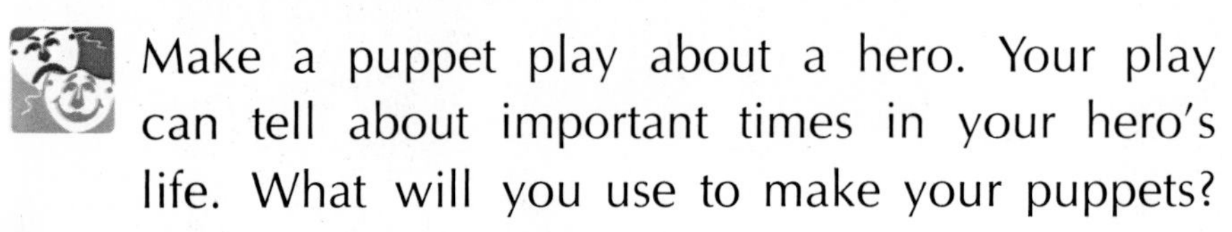

Make a puppet play about a hero. Your play can tell about important times in your hero's life. What will you use to make your puppets?

Self Study

1. Some rules are made by people in government. Some rules are made by parents. Teachers make rules. People make rules for themselves. What is one of the best rules you know? When do you think a rule is a good rule? How can rules be changed if people don't like them?

2. You can make up rules for yourself. What do you believe in? What code do you want to live by? What rules will you make up for yourself now? Do you think you will ever change the rules you make now?

What way of deciding does each picture show?

Ways of Deciding

Do you know this poem?

One potato, two potato,
Three potato, four,
Five potato, six potato,
Seven potato, MORE!

Each person's fist counts as a "potato." If your fist gets counted as "More," you must put it behind your back. Then the poem is said again and again. If both fists become "More," you are *it*.

Do you think One Potato is a fair way to decide who is *it*? Why or why not?

Many children use Jankenpon (JAN·kun·PUN) to decide who will be *it*. Here are the rules.

The players put their hands behind them. They say, together, "Jan-ken-pon!" Then they bring their hands forward.

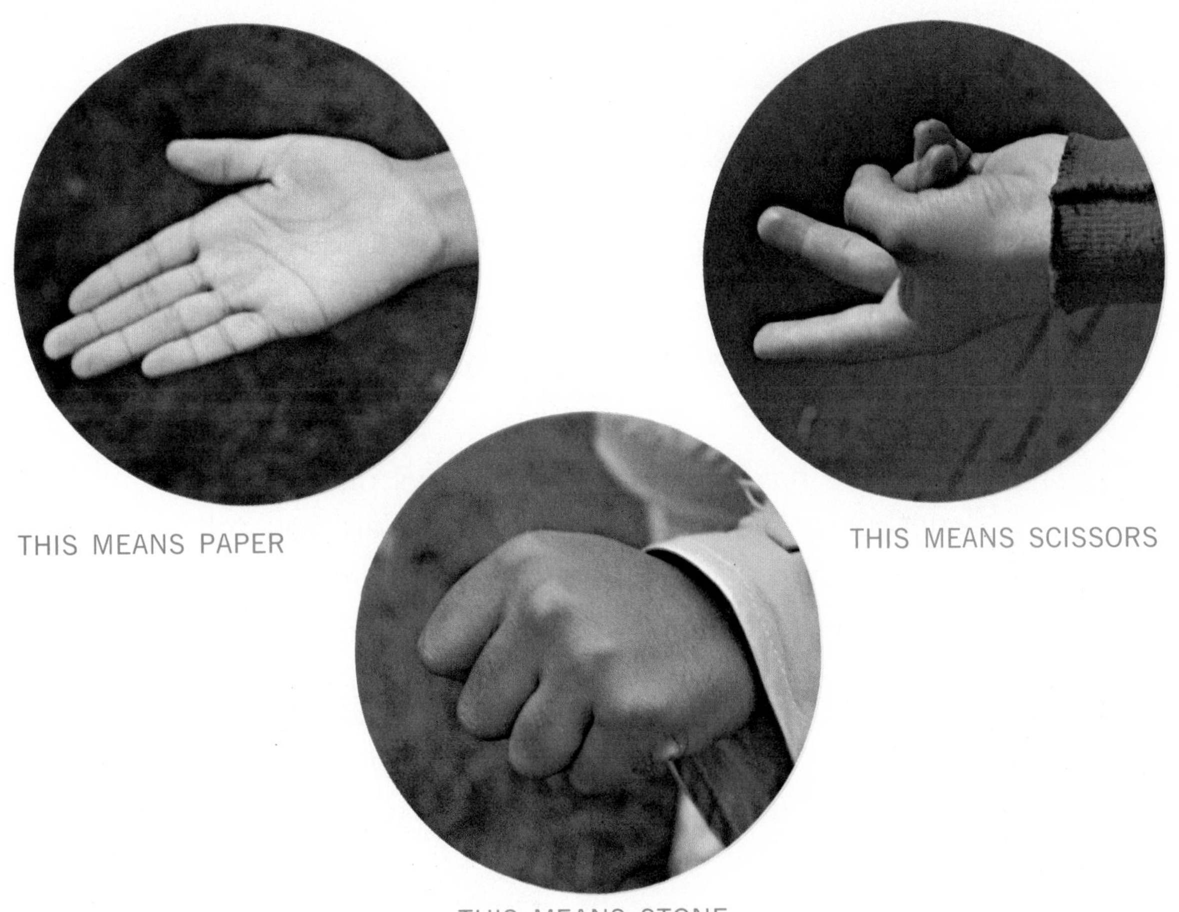

THIS MEANS PAPER

THIS MEANS SCISSORS

THIS MEANS STONE

Stone wins over scissors. Scissors win over paper. Paper wins over stone. This is because rock breaks scissors. Scissors cut paper. Paper covers rock.

Which game do you think is fairer? What is a fair way to decide who is *it*?

Deciding Questions

Games are often decided by luck. Suppose all questions were decided by luck. How fair would that be?

People have many different ways of deciding questions. Look at each picture. Can you tell who is the person who decides? What do you think that person is saying?

Who decides if a *law* has been broken? That is one of the most important questions people have to decide. A law is a rule followed by a group of people. Laws help people live in peace.

In many countries today people know the laws. They can find out how and why the laws were made. The pictures show some of the ways people try to change laws.

Trials and Tournaments

Many years ago in Europe, people believed that *trial by combat* was a good way to decide who had broken the law. In those days, a trial meant a test. Combat is fighting. In trial by combat, people believed that God would help the person who was right.

Stories say that King Arthur tried to do away with so much fighting. He set up games where people could fight in fun, not to kill the other person. These games were called *tournaments* (TUR·nuh·munts). The pictures show two games played at tournaments.

Today, sports tournaments are based on the same idea. People like to play against one another in sports. What sport do you like best? Why do you like it?

Who decides today if a law has been broken? In most states a judge or a group of men and women called a *jury* (JOOR·ee) decides. Before the trial, the jury promises to decide the facts fairly. The jury listens carefully to both sides of the case. They then tell the judge what they think the facts are. In some trials, all of the people on a jury must agree that a law has been broken. In other trials, nine out of twelve people must agree.

Do you think that a jury trial is a fair way to decide?

Castles for Safety

Long ago in Europe, many rich people lived in great castles like these. These people were afraid someone might steal from them. They wanted to feel safe in their homes.

Some people decided to have their castles built on hills. Other people had ditches full of water all around their castles. Such ditches are called *moats* (MOHTS). A heavy wooden bridge could be lowered down across the ditch. Most of the time the bridge was up. People felt safer that way. Why would a hill or a moat help people feel safer?

Castles were built of stone and had high walls. The walls were so thick that rooms were built in them. Many castles had no windows. You can see that this one has little openings in the walls. Knights would shoot arrows at the enemy through these openings.

You can see that a castle was built for safety. Are houses today built for safety? Are they built for comfort? Are they built for beauty?

Suppose you had no one to fear. Suppose everyone were your friend. Would you still lock your door? What kind of house would you build if you had no one to fear?

SELF EXPRESSION

The children in the pictures at the top are building *model* castles. A model castle looks like a real castle, but it is very small. These castles are built for people who are about as tall as elves. Can you tell what the children are using to make their castles?

The children in the lower pictures are building houses of peace. They are making houses for people who have nothing to fear. Some of the houses they made don't even have any walls!

You can make a castle or a house of peace. You can paint a picture or build a model.

Before you begin, think how the building would be used if it were real. Think about the family that might live there. What would the family need? Make a building or a castle that the family would like.

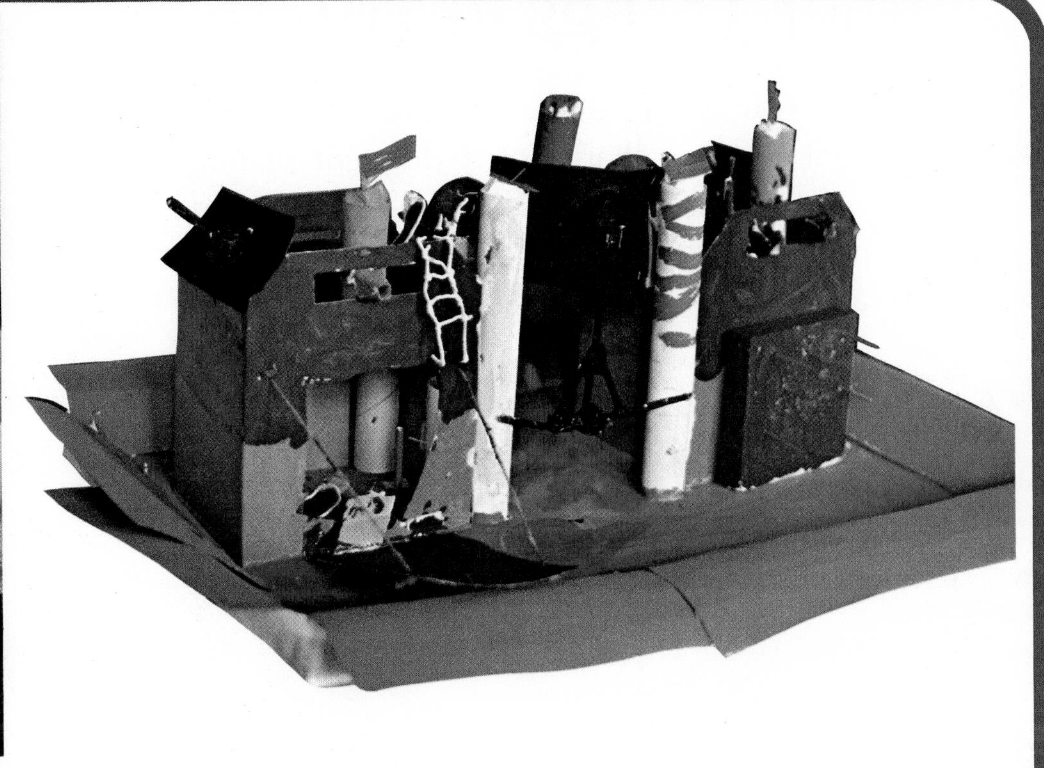

Other Things to Try

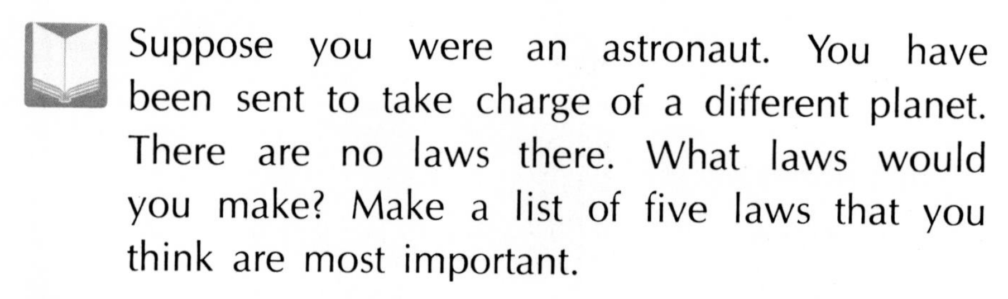

Suppose you were an astronaut. You have been sent to take charge of a different planet. There are no laws there. What laws would you make? Make a list of five laws that you think are most important.

Make up a story about a hero. You can tell a true story or make up a story. Then find music that goes with the different parts of your story. You can make up music if you like. How will you share your musical story?

Self Study

1 Today, some people fear poor drivers. Others fear air pollution. What are you afraid of? Why do you fear these things? How can you protect yourself from the things you fear?

2 You may have seen movies about knights. You may have read stories about the Round Table. Why are people still telling stories about knights? Some day perhaps you, too, will do a great deed. What would you like people in the year 2050 to say about you?

OUR MASTERPIECE

Here I am at my school. I am showing my friends what I've made. The man in the art store wants to sell some of my things. He will put them in his window. There will be a sign on them, "Handcrafted by Benita Terrell." "Handcrafted" means I made them by hand.

Here I am with my dad. The show is about to begin. I don't feel so scared now. This is the moment I've been waiting for all year.

Now we are in the parade. That's my mom ahead of us. The lights are so bright. I can't see the people. But I can hear them. Everyone is clapping. I'm a real clown at last!

Dad and I are playing together. He needed an accordion player for a Christmas show. I love to play for people. Sometimes little kids ask me how long I've been playing. They can't believe it's just one year.

Now I'm playing guitar with some friends. Maybe some day I will play as well as my dad. I know I have far to go. He says I have made a good start.

We are dancing for all the kids in school. We are doing a dance I made up. I feel good when I'm dancing. I can remember all the steps easily most of the time.

Now we are dancing for our mothers and fathers. Dad says he is glad I am so good at dancing. He says, "Everyone should do at least one thing very well. You, my son, can now dance well. You may choose to do something else next year. Whatever you do, I know you will do your best."

I am at the Fair. The judges are deciding who will be the winner. They have asked me all kinds of questions about horses. They said they can see I have taken good care of Rusty. He is such a beautiful horse.

He won! We won! Here is my prize. He was judged Champion of the Breed. I knew all along that he was a champion. Dad says I will be a champion too some day.

THEN AND NOW

There were no telephones in the pueblo when my mom was ten years old. When they wanted to talk to somebody, they had to go to that person's home. There were no notices delivered to the houses. They had to rely on a town crier for information of importance. My mom's family didn't subscribe to a daily newspaper or magazine.

Now we have telephones which we get information from. We alsooget information from newspapers, magazines and television.

Here is part of something I wrote. I wrote about my mother. I wrote about her life when she was ten years old. Then I wrote about my life now. Maybe I will write a book about this.

Here is a show of some pictures I took. Will I write or take pictures when I grow up? I can't decide. Mom and Dad say there is plenty of time. Some day I want to be really good at something. Mom says, "Whatever you become, we will love you. The most important thing to become is a good person. And you have made the best start on that."

WORDS TO KNOW

You may already know the meaning of many of these words. They are all words that are worth learning. You will be meeting them many times.

Sometimes a word has more than one meaning. Just the meaning that is used here is given.

A page number follows each word. It tells where you will find more about the word.

accent (AK·sent), a heavier or stronger note or color than those around it. 177

celebration (sel·uh·BRAY·shun), a joyful party or happy time. **Celebrations** often honor people or holidays. 81

ceremony (SAYR·uh·moh·nee), an act that must be done in a certain way. When people become citizens, they take part in a **ceremony.** 134

chant, a simple tune. The melody may be all on one pitch or perhaps have two or three pitches. The same pattern of notes is repeated over and over in a **chant.** 76

character (KAR·ik·tur), a person in a play or a story. 14

code, a set of signs or marks used to send a message, 96; a set or rules or laws. 251

composer (kum·POH·zur), someone who makes up music. 88

craft, an art or a job that takes training to do. **Craft** often means skill, being able to do something well. 185

decorate, to make more beautiful by adding colors and patterns. 50

exaggerate (ig·ZAJ·uh·rayt), to make bigger or greater in size or importance than a person would expect. 12

faith, trust, being able to depend on a person or thing. 188

hero, a person of great courage. **Hero** may mean either a man or a woman admired by many people. A woman **hero** may be called a **heroine.** 249

imagination (i·ma·juh·NAY·shun), the power to make up new ideas, stories, music. 130

imitate (IM·uh·tayt), to act or to try to act in the same way as another person. 78

instrument, a tool used in any kind of work. In this book, **instrument** often means something used to make musical sounds. An accordion, a guitar, and a piano are **instruments.** 16

invent, to make up for the first time. 138

justice, fairness, by the rules of right and wrong. 254

landscape, a picture showing nature on land. 64

law, a rule that tells how a group of people should act. 263

masterpiece, the greatest or best thing done by the person who made it. 188

melody (MEL·uh·dee), a tune, a pattern of musical tones that sounds pleasant. 46

mime (MIYM), to play a part with hand and body movements, not using words. A person who does pantomime is called a **mime.** 30

mural (MYOOR·uhl), a painting on a ceiling or wall. 202

museum (myoo·ZEE·um), a building that has in it works of art, science, or nature. 118

pantomime (PAN·tuh·miym), to act without using words. Mime is a short form of **pantomime.** 9

pattern, a way of arranging colors, sounds, numbers, or anything else so that at least one of them repeats in a regular way. 88

pitch, a tone in music. 39

proverb (PROV·urb), a very old saying that tells what a group of people believe. 197

rhythm (RI·thum), a regular arrangement of stronger and weaker sounds, accents, colors, or movements in music, poetry, art, and dance. 47, 176

skill, ability to do something easily and well. 109

style, the way in which something is done. 231

symbol (SIM·buhl), a mark or sign that stands for something else. 96

B 5
C 6
D 7
E 8
F 9
G 0
H 1
I 2
J 3